SQUARE PIE GUY

SQUARE PIE GUY

DETROIT-STYLE PIZZA AT HOME

MARC SCHECHTER

GABI MOSKOWITZ

weldonowen

CONTENTS

NEW CLASSICS

OUT OF THE BOX

FOREWORD

There are people who, without even trying to, make other people's lives richer. Not through big statements, but through a relentless belief in something that matters. Marc is one of those people.

When I started Gozney, I wasn't building a brand. I was twenty-one, fresh out of rehab, and searching for direction. What I found was purpose. Not just pizza, but what is created around it. Connection. Community. A sense of belonging. It gave me a North Star.

Marc found his North Star the same way. What started with a Roccbox oven and an obsession became something far bigger. Not just a number of remarkable restaurants, but a community and a point of view that people want to be part of. For me, he never set out to build a business. He set out to get the pizza right. Everything else followed.

That same spirit runs through this book. *Square Pie Guy* isn't just about making great pizza. It's about understanding it. Where it comes from, how it evolves, and why it matters. Marc respects the craft but has the confidence to question it, push it, and reimagine it. That's what makes his food and this book feel alive. What matters most to me isn't the scale of what Marc has built. It's what his story unlocks in other people. It proves that you don't need permission, credentials, or the perfect plan. You just need to care enough to start and to keep going. I'm proud that a Gozney oven played a small role at the beginning of this journey. But everything that followed, that's all Marc.

Tom Gozney, Founder and CEO of Gozney

GOZNEY
LA
sourdough

INTRODUCTION

Before I tell you how I fell in love with Detroit-style pizza, there's something you should know about me: I really don't like being told what to do. Especially when it's framed as something I *can't* do. If you tell me it's impossible, I will reorganize my entire life just to prove you wrong. I've always been this way—just ask my Hebrew school teachers (who very nearly sent me home for starting a small, spirited uprising involving ham).

I graduated from college with a marketing degree, moved to Astoria, Queens, and landed a job in sales. If you didn't know, sales is a rough road. When you're up, you're golden. When you're down, you learn exactly what "you're only as good as your last sale" really means. Work was stressful, so I needed a creative outlet, which led me to sign up for a stand-up comedy class on a whim. I quickly found myself hooked, and even when my day job drained the life out of me, I lived for the nights I got to be onstage.

Then I met a girl. She was smart, beautiful, and successful, and when she got a big job offer in Seattle, I followed her across the country. I left behind my friends, family, and comedy side hustle (albeit one that paid mostly in drink tickets), convinced that chasing traditional success would make me a worthy partner. We got engaged. She got into grad school, so we moved to Berkeley. She was busy with school, but I was lonely and a little bored. I can see now that things were starting to unravel, but I wasn't ready to admit it to myself or anyone else.

Around that time, I was helping my childhood friend Jeff—an actual chef—move into a new apartment. While unpacking his kitchen, I pulled a weathered pizza cookbook out of a box. The pie on the cover was mouthwatering, and I asked if I could borrow it. "You can have it," he said, tossing in a pizza stone and peel for good measure. Then he added, almost offhandedly, "Just don't expect to make restaurant-quality pizza at home. It's impossible."

That was it. The challenge was planted. Despite my lukewarm interest in cooking and profound hatred of doing dishes, something in me lit up. I didn't just want to try making pizza at home, I *needed* to.

My first pies using Jeff's offloaded book and cookware were . . . not great. They were patchy, uneven, and structurally unsound. But even so, they were delicious and I was obsessed. That I, with my crappy apartment oven and beginner-level skills, had the power to turn cheap ingredients into something this good was absolutely mind-blowing to me. I tore through every pizza book I could find—*The Pizza Bible* by Tony Gemignani, *The Elements of Pizza* by Ken Forkish, *Pizza Camp* by Joe Beddia—and started throwing pizza parties for our new California friends. As I practiced, my pies gradually improved, and I realized I was beginning to find my groove again, in the kitchen, at least, if not necessarily in life. One day, in a fit of homesickness, I bought a few high-edged steel Detroit-style pans so I could attempt to re-create the thick, cheesy Sicilian slices from Gino's of Great Neck, the pizzeria I grew up eating at. When I finally nailed that first one, it felt like I'd cracked a sacred code.

Then, the wedding engagement ended—messily and somewhat predictably. Devastated and dejected, I moved out. The only thing that made me feel okay during that time, even briefly, was making pizza. It grounded me, connected me to home, and reminded me that simple things—flour, water, cheese—can become something greater when you give them a little attention, a little care, and some time to do their thing.

So I kept going. I spent my nights staging (translation of the French term for interning in a professional kitchen) at some of the top pizzerias in the Bay Area while still working my day job. I learned how to mix dough in a machine the size of a small refrigerator, how to fail, how to recover. I ran a pizza pop-up in a wine bar that started off as a disaster but slowly, stubbornly found its rhythm. One night, a couple asked me to cater their wedding with Detroit-style pizza. I told them I didn't have enough pans, and they told me to put the pans in the quote. I did. They said yes. And just like that, I owned thirty pans by LloydPans and had the seed money for what would become Square Pie Guys.

From there, things grew. Pop-ups turned into a restaurant. Square Pie Guys opened its first location in the SoMa neighborhood of San Francisco. We opened more locations, hired more people, continued to grow, and now I'm here, telling you all about it in this book. It was hard—it still is. But it's also the best thing I've ever done.

I love my friend Jeff, but he was wrong, by the way. You *can* make restaurant-quality pizza at home, especially Detroit-style. You don't need fancy gear. You just need a pan, a few ingredients, and a little guidance, and that's why I wrote this book. To show you that it's not only possible, it's wildly doable and utterly delicious. I hope you have as much fun cooking from it as much as I did writing it.

Love and pizza,

MARC

P.S. I did eventually meet someone new: Tess. On our first date, I ordered us an 18-inch pizza to share. A big commitment, for sure, but when I met her, I knew I was ready.

P.P.S. Reader, I married her.

ORGANIC BREAD FLOUR
CENTRAL MILLING
CUP4CUP
MULTIPURPOSE FLOU
GLUTEN FREE
BUT YOU'D NEVER KNOW IT
UNBLEACHED
EAD FLOUR
RGANIC
5 LBS (2.27kg)
USDA ORGANIC
Bread Flour
Semolina
SINCE 1886
DIAMON
CRYSTA
SALT CO
KOSHE
SALT FLAKES

SQUARE ONE

You Say Pizza, We Say Pie

So, what exactly makes a pizza Detroit-style?

The legend goes that Detroit-style pizza was first invented in 1946 at a diner called Buddy's Rendezvous Pizzeria in Detroit on Six Mile Road. There's some disagreement about exactly whose recipe for sfincione, a focaccia-like Sicilian pizza, owners Gus and Anna Guerra were trying to make (sources say it was either Anna's mother's or one of their employees'), but the gist is that they lacked both the proper pan and fresh mozzarella and needed to improvise. They got a blue steel drip pan from a nearby automobile factory (the kind used to hold small car parts) and Wisconsin brick cheese (a white, tangy semihard cheese, like a mashup of low-moisture mozzarella and cheddar) and did their best to re-create the original. They spooned the sauce on top of the baked pie instead of putting it under the cheese, cut it into squares, and the resulting pie immediately won over their customers.

Now, all these years later, Buddy's remains the OG mothership for Detroit-style pizza aficionados.

Today, Detroit-style pizza is served all over the Midwest and is increasingly available across the country, especially in recent years. We're experiencing something of a heyday, and for good reason: You get a crust that's sturdy and almost buttery on the outside and light and airy inside, with a caramelized cheese crown (called the frico, it's a major component of what makes Detroit-style pizza so un-put-down-able), a substantial layer of cheese that is browned and bubbly on top, but gooey enough to achieve serious cheese-pulls just beneath, plus a lightly sweet, oregano-kissed sauce.

These days, you can buy a Detroit-style pizza pan instead of having to borrow one from your local car assembly line, and you can find brick cheese, mozzarella, or whatever type of cheese you like at your local supermarket. Still, I like to think the rebellious nature of Detroit pizza's origins permeates the style to this day. Detroit-style pizza says, "Screw the pizza rules, make me on your own terms," which I love because, as I've established, I'm not really into rules. As a chef and restaurant owner, I think this gives me an edge; I'm not afraid to color outside the lines, try new things, or break tradition. Not everyone agrees with my perspective, though.

On one of the first days of dinner service at Square Pie Guys' first location, I was stopping by tables, checking in with customers about how they liked their food. My queries had largely been met with raves and assurances from diners that they'd be back as soon as possible, but when I walked up to a table where two women and one man were eating and asked them how they liked everything, I was not prepared for what I would hear.

"I'm from Detroit," one of the women told me. "Are you?"

"No," I answered tentatively. I wasn't exactly sure where this was going, but I had the distinct feeling she wasn't just curious if I knew someone she'd gone to summer camp with. "I'm originally from New York."

"Uh-huh," she said flatly, looking at me like I'd just confirmed I was the kind of person who claps when airplanes land. "Well, ***I'm*** from Detroit, and this is not Detroit-style pizza. You're appropriating my hometown's food, and honestly, it pisses me off."

I was floored. Unsure what else to say, I apologized, told her I hadn't thought about it that way, and said I hoped she could still enjoy her meal.

For folks who share her sentiment, the pies in the Old-School Pies chapter are a little closer to what you'd find in Detroit, but I still take some liberties with them. I don't like marinara as the top layer of my pizza—upside down style, as I grew up saying, or with a "red top," as it is also known—and I'm not wild about brick cheese, either. I prefer a pie with a cheddar crust and mozzarella over the top. Is that textbook Detroit-style? Well, no. Does it capture the spirit of the style and taste damn delicious? I—and the hundreds of thousands of people who frequent Square Pie Guys' many locations—would say yes.

Since my first conversation with that disappointed Detroiter, I've had some version of it with Detroit-style purists dozens of times and received countless Yelp reviews from diners who were somewhere on the annoyed-to-incensed spectrum that we don't put marinara on top of our pies after baking, the way they do in the Midwest. And look, I get it. Tradition is emotionally loaded. When a food is near and dear to your heart, you don't necessarily want someone messing with it.

But if there's one thing I've learned in the pizza business—and in life—it's that things work better when you keep your eyes on your own paper. When you make decisions based exclusively on what you think other people want, you cut yourself off from your internal compass, the one that guides you toward what you know in your bones is right for you. Detroit-style pizza doesn't try to compete with deep dish or New York–style or Napoli, and I don't try to compete with the culinary memories of someone's southeast Michigan childhood. I believe that, at its heart, Detroit-style pizza is a celebration of innovation—it's about applying good techniques to the ingredients and equipment you have access to, even when the results defy tradition. Even when they're a little bit out there. Even when—and occasionally I might argue ***because***—they piss off traditionalists.

Recommended Tools and Equipment

People often ask me what they need to buy to start making Detroit-style pizza at home. "***A scale, dummy!***" is usually the first thing out of my mouth (more on that later), but then I regain my composure and try to answer the question.

My answer depends on how much they seem to enjoy shopping for kitchen gear. On one hand, the right tools do make things better and easier and help you avoid unnecessary frustration. Everything on this list is something I personally own (in triplicate, in several cases) and can confirm will make your pizza-making experience smoother and your results better.

That said, if you can't or don't want to buy any of it, you can almost certainly still make excellent square pies with whatever is already lurking in your kitchen cabinets. You need a bowl, a spoon, a cheese grater, and something oven-safe to bake it in, preferably made of metal. Unless your kitchen is functionally just a microwave and a bottle of expired ranch, you're probably more prepared than you think. But if you want to really do it right, I've got some opinions. Because, as I've said, I do believe you don't need too much special equipment to make great Detroit pies, I've organized this list to help you build your tool kit gradually. There's a basic list for Pizza Fans—that is, folks who are newer to pizza-making and aren't quite sure if they're ready to commit. If you're more of a Pizza Aficionado—meaning that maybe you aren't completely obsessed with Detroit-style pizza (yet!), but it's part of your regular rotation, get everything on the Pizza Fans list, plus the next set of items. And for ***my*** people, the total Pizza Nerds who have a name for their sourdough starter and daydream about baker's percentages and toppings combinations? You're gonna want the whole shebang, everything on all three lists.

LEVEL 1: PIZZA FAN
Casual Pizza Maker

Mixing bowls: If you cook a lot, you probably already have a set of these. If not, buy a sturdy set of stainless steel ones, preferably from a restaurant supply store (no need for them to be expensive), and get multiple sizes between 1 and 5 quarts.

Cheese grater: Cheese you grate yourself is cheaper, melts more evenly, and tastes light-years better than the additive-filled, anti-caking-agent-coated pre-shredded variety. A metal box grater works well, or use the grater attachment on your food processor to grate a lot of cheese in literal seconds.

Plastic wrap (or lids that fit on your mixing bowls and pans): Detroit pizza dough goes through multiple resting periods before it's ready to use—first in the mixing bowl, then again in the pan, and it's important to cover your dough both times. If your mixing bowl set has fitted lids, use those; just make sure it's an airtight seal. If not, opt for plastic wrap. Same goes for your pans. LloydPans makes lids for its pans, which can be purchased on the company's website or from larger retailers like Amazon.

Thin metal spatula: Getting a cooked Detroit pie out of a pan can be a little tricky at first, but you'll get the hang of it. I like to use a thin metal spatula (like a fish spatula) to gently separate it from the edge of the pan, then lift it onto a board or cooling rack. You could also use a cake lifter, a large offset icing spatula, or any other large, thin spatula to loosen the sides and lift the pie out. One other trick is to tilt your pizza pan and use a fork to drag the pizza onto a baking sheet, cutting board, or cooling rack.

LEVEL 2: PIZZA AFICIONADO
Dedicated Home Pizza Maker

Digital scale: This is one gadget I feel strongly about. You should really consider getting one, okay? Honestly, you seem really cool. Can I be frank? Yeah? You're sure? Okay, here I go. HAVING A DIGITAL SCALE IS NONNEGOTIABLE! CLOSE THIS BOOK AND GO BUY ONE RIGHT NOW!

Sorry to scream at you. I get a little, shall we say, emotional about digital kitchen scales. See page 22 for more, and I'll be right here doing the breathing exercises my therapist recommended. See page 23 for why. You can still make pizza without one, but having one makes a big difference in both your experience of dough-making and the results of your efforts.

Detroit pizza pan: Do you technically need a pan made specifically for Detroit-style pizza? No. But . . . if you're serious about making Detroit-style pizza, please allow me to gently recommend that you purchase the real deal. The most popular brand (and the one we use in the store) is LloydPans. If you don't have or don't want to buy a Detroit-style pizza pan, use another metal pan, preferably stainless steel, aluminum, or cast iron, even if it's round. Cake pans, casserole dishes, and rimmed sheet pans will all work, even if the final results are a little different from what you'd get in a proper Detroit-style pizza pan. (See page 20 for more information.) But seriously? Come on, buddy. You bought the fucking book. You made dough, you grated a metric fuck-ton of cheese. Don't sell yourself short and dump it into any old pan. The real ones are not that expensive, and you can use them for other stuff, too. Like lasagna. Don't you like lasagna? What's that? You're trying to save money? Fine. I can respect that. Maybe you can be my financial planner because you're clearly better at saving money than I am. Use whatever pan you've got, I guess—but promise me you'll at least consider getting a Lloyd.

Nonabrasive sponge and mild dish soap: If you're using a Detroit-style pizza pan, it's important to take good care of it, and that means not scrubbing. Wash it with water and mild dish soap and soak it to remove any baked-on cheese or sauce. After soaking, gently loosen any crud with a spatula, then wipe clean with a sponge. Keep steel wool and the like far, far away.

LEVEL 3: PIZZA NERD
Obsessed Pizzaiolo

Stand mixer: The 2-Day Dough (page 36), which I use most often, and which we use at the restaurant, the Long Weekend Dough (page 38), and the Gluten-Free Dough (page 41) can all absolutely be made by hand. But there's no denying that it's a lot less labor-intensive and cleaner to make them in a stand mixer. Whatever you've got will do, and if you're looking to buy one, I recommend a KitchenAid 6-quart Bowl Lift Stand Mixer.

Food processor, immersion blender, or high-powered blender: A high-powered food processor (like a Cuisinart) is great for pulsing or pureeing sauces like pesto or creamy vodka sauce, but it's also a nice tool for mixing dough if you don't have a stand mixer. An immersion blender, sometimes also called a hand blender or a stick blender, is extremely convenient in that you can puree sauces (along with soups and dips, too) right in their mixing or cooking container without having to transfer them to the bowl of a food processor. If you have lots of space and cook frequently, both are nice to have, but if you have room for only one, go for the immersion blender.

Pizza stone and peel: Baking your Detroit-style pizza in its pan, directly on a stone, ensures even heat distribution and a perfectly crisp crust. A peel makes transferring pizzas in and out of the oven effortless and precise. Plus, both tools are versatile enough to use for other breads, like round pizza (page 135), ciabatta (page 131), pitas, and more.

A Note About Alternative Pans

Like I said: You don't have to buy a bunch of new gear to make great Detroit-style pies at home. While I swear by LloydPans for that perfect high-walled, cheese-crusted, crispy-bottomed result, other pans will absolutely work—you just might need to tweak your approach a bit or accept that the outcome will be slightly different. Still good. Still pizza. Just a slightly different personality.

Some tips for using common kitchen stand-ins:

- **RIMMED HALF-SHEET TRAY:** Half-sheet trays, also known as rimmed baking sheets, are generally 18 by 13 inches, bigger overall and less deep than a Detroit pan. Rather than scale up your dough, I recommend just accepting that your pie will be a little thinner because the pan's shallowness creates a thinner crust that lands somewhere between a Detroit pizza and a grandma pie and makes a pizza you can serve in neat little squares at a party. It's not exactly traditional, but it works. I recommend parbaking the crust for 5 to 6 minutes first—it'll shrink a bit—and then fill in the gaps with cheese for a proper frico edge.

- **12-INCH CAST-IRON SKILLET:** Sure, it's round. But it holds heat like a champ and delivers a killer crust. Its surface area is smaller than a 10-by-14-inch pan, so use four-fifths of the dough recipe (and throw the rest into something fun from the Out of the Box chapter, page 128). Plus, it looks rustic and impressive, in a flannel-shirt-I-live-in-a-cabin-I-built-myself-and-and-know-how-to-chop-wood kind of way.

- **9-BY-13-INCH (OR SIMILAR) METAL CAKE PAN:** This one's closer to a proper Detroit-style shape. The crust will be slightly thicker than usual, but you'll get decent edge caramelization and a good bake. Just make sure it's metal. Glass pan = soggy bottom.

Square Pie Pantry

If you're anything like me, once you start making square pies at home, you'll catch the bug—and suddenly your fridge will start looking suspiciously pizza-prepped at all times. Below are the core ingredients I reach for when I'm making pies, whether at home or at the shop. Think of this list the same way you'd think of the Recommended Tools and Equipment section: helpful, not mandatory. Just aim for the best version of each that fits your budget and pantry space.

Flour: Yes, you can absolutely use the all-purpose flour that's been hanging out in your cabinet since your quarantine banana bread phase. It'll work just fine. That said, I prefer bread flour—it's higher in protein, which gives the crust a chewier bite and a little more structure. At the restaurant, we use Red Rose flour from Central Milling in Sonoma County (fancy, I know), but you don't need to track it down unless you want to. King Arthur bread flour is very solid and widely available at most grocery stores.

Yeast: If it's alive, it'll work. I use instant yeast because it doesn't need to be dissolved in water first, which makes things easier. But if you've got active dry yeast instead, that's fine too—just stir it into the water before adding it to your dough and carry on. Don't overthink it.

Salt: You'd be surprised how much salt matters. It helps control fermentation (aka how wild your dough gets), which impacts your crust's structure. Plus, it makes everything taste like actual food. Like almost every other restaurant, we use Diamond Crystal kosher salt at the restaurant, and it's what I use in all the recipes here, which you'll see I've indicated in each one. Diamond Kosher is easy to measure and pinch out of a bowl, it's not too salty, and it dissolves quickly. If you're using table salt, sea salt, or anything else, you'll likely need to adjust the amount, because other salts pack more saltiness by volume, which can throw off the final product.

If you can't find Diamond Crystal or prefer to use other salt, see below for a handy conversion table based on quantities frequently called for in the recipes in this book.

Tomatoes: I use canned, crushed San Marzano tomatoes in my sauce recipes at home and at the shop. Personally, I'm a fan of Bianco DiNapoli, but just get the best-tasting ones you can reasonably afford. Some people insist on using only Italian-grown tomatoes, like that's the only place in the world where tomatoes know how to grow. I live in California—our produce is incredible. Good tomatoes are good tomatoes. Use what tastes great to you and don't get hung up on the passport.

SALT TYPE	0.7 GRAM	3 GRAMS	6 GRAMS
Diamond Crystal kosher salt	¼ teaspoon	1 teaspoon	2 teaspoons
Morton kosher salt	scant ⅛ teaspoon	½ teaspoon	1 teaspoon
table salt	scant ⅛ teaspoon	½ teaspoon	1 teaspoon
fine Himalayan pink salt	scant ⅛ teaspoon	½ teaspoon	1 teaspoon
fine sea salt	scant ⅛ teaspoon	½ teaspoon	1 teaspoon
coarse sea salt	⅛ teaspoon	¾ teaspoon	1½ teaspoons

Cheese: There are a few different cheeses in this book's recipes, and quality really does matter. If you can spring for the good stuff, do it. At the shop, we use whole-milk low-moisture mozzarella, fresh whole-milk mozzarella, Tillamook medium cheddar, and Grana Padano to finish our pies. This is not the time for part-skim or "lite" anything (honestly, when is?).

One more thing—and I feel ***strongly*** about it: Whatever you do, buy blocks of cheese and dice or grate it yourself. Yes, I know it's annoying. But pre-shredded cheese is coated with cellulose so that it doesn't clump, which also means it doesn't melt the way you want it to. The crust won't be as lacy, and the cheese won't be as gooey. Trust me, just dice or shred the cheese.

Gluten-free flour: If you're going gluten-free, I can't recommend Cup4Cup enough. It was developed by Chef Thomas Keller, and it's kind of a miracle. It bakes up almost indistinguishably from regular flour. It's what we use for the gluten-free dough at the shop and what I use at home when I cook for Tess. It's not the cheapest, but if you're serious about texture and flavor, it's worth the splurge.

Dairy-free cheese: I like Violife's vegan mozzarella and cheddar. They melt like real cheese and taste pretty close to the real thing. Will it fool your grandma from Wisconsin? Maybe not. But for dairy-free pizza, it does the job and then some.

Vegan meat: Field Roast makes a surprisingly legit vegan pepperoni. Drizzle it with a little olive oil before baking to re-create that greasy, glorious vibe of the real stuff. For fake sausage and chicken, I like Beyond Meat and Impossible. One pro move: Bake the Impossible chicken nuggets first, then slice them up and use them on pies like the Szechuan Chicken (page 114) or Buffalo Chicken (page 119), or on a Vodka Chicken Parm Sandwich (page 137). Shockingly good, and even the meat eaters won't complain.

Use a F*cking Scale

A Brief Rant

I'm a pretty chill guy. Easygoing. Hard to rattle (Tess ***fully*** agrees with this, ***right, babe??***). Unless I'm driving. (Great Neck may technically be on Long Island, but I was raised with a full NYC quota of road rage.) Still, I don't yell. I don't hit. I can respectfully disagree like the mature, civilized adult I am.

Except when it comes to measuring ingredients.

If you're baking—or making pizza dough—and you're not using a digital scale, I have one question: Why do you ***hate*** yourself? Do you ***want*** dense crusts, lumpy batter, and the existential despair that comes from watching your dough refuse to rise? Because that's what happens when you scoop flour with a cup. Most of the time I'll tell you that Detroit-style pizza doesn't require fancy tools. You can use a sheet pan or a cast-iron skillet. Your oven can be a beat-up rental special. But I will die on the hill of the digital kitchen scale. It's cheap, it's accurate, and it will make you a better cook instantly.

Look, it's not your fault. You were misled—by cookbooks, blogs, and the ghosts of home-ec teachers past, all telling you to level flour with a butter knife like it's 1953. But baking by volume is a fool's errand. A "heaping cup"? A "scant tablespoon"? What does that even mean? Measuring by volume is like guessing someone's weight by how loud their footsteps sound, and that's a bad idea for a lot of reasons.

A scale is not expensive. Go ahead. Open your phone. Search "digital kitchen scale" on your shopping app of choice. You'll find a solid one for less than what you paid for that overpriced latte you're drinking while reading this. It'll be at your doorstep in two days, and your future self will want to French-kiss you for it.

STILL SCARED? HERE'S HOW TO USE IT:

1. TURN IT ON.
2. SET YOUR BOWL ON IT. HIT "ZERO."
3. ADD AN INGREDIENT UNTIL THE NUMBER MATCHES THE RECIPE.
4. HIT "ZERO" AGAIN. ADD THE NEXT ONE.
5. REPEAT UNTIL DONE.

THAT'S IT. NO MEASURING CUPS, NO SPOONS, NO CLEANUP MOUNTAIN. JUST ONE BOWL. ONE BUTTON. AND PERFECT RESULTS EVERY TIME.

SO, NO—YOU DON'T HAVE TO USE A SCALE FOR THE RECIPES IN THIS BOOK. I'VE INCLUDED CUP AND SPOON MEASUREMENTS BECAUSE I'M NOT A TOTAL MONSTER.

BUT IF YOU WANT CONSISTENT DOUGH, IF YOU WANT FLUFFY INSIDES AND CRISPY OUTSIDES AND BRAGGING RIGHTS FOR DAYS—USE THE F*CKING SCALE.

WE'RE GOOD NOW. I'M GLAD WE HAD THIS TALK.

Create Your Own Pie

With a Few Caveats

Every pizza recipe in this book is the result of months (sometimes years) of trial and error, so I really do hope you'll make them all as written. But look, I'm the owner of a pizzeria. I know people have their preferences when it comes to pizza, the toppings and combinations they hold close to their hearts, and I understand that it's my job to help make the toppings-related dreams of anyone who eats in my pie shop come true. I love it when people get creative with toppings, because pizza is supposed to be fun and reflective of what tastes good to you.

But I also know how easy it is to seriously screw up a beautiful crust by topping it poorly, so in this section, I'd like to respectfully, ***lovingly*** offer some gentle guidance for when you decide to throw caution and all the research and development my kitchen team and I have done to the wind, and design your own Detroit pie.

1. The main thing to keep in mind is that, while I understand it's tempting to load up on everything you like, less really is more when it comes to toppings quantity. Detroit-style pies can handle a bit more sauce, cheese, and toppings than their thinner Neapolitan or New York–style sisters, but even so, going overboard can turn your pie into a soupy bread bowl, which is not what we're going for. You want a thin layer of sauce, and the cheese should go across the surface of the pizza, but you should still be able to peep little pockets of the sauce beneath. We're making pizza here, not lasagna.

2. In general (and there are exceptions), I don't put more than three types of toppings (beyond sauce and cheese) on my Detroit pies. Between crust, sauce, and cheese, you're already working with a lot of flavor, and when too much is going on toppings-wise, it can be hard to appreciate any of it.

3. Too much moisture ruins a pie. If you're using an ingredient that contains a lot of water (like mushrooms, zucchini, or pine-apple), I recommend cooking at least some of the water out first so it doesn't drench your pizza and make it soggy.

4. Resist the urge to dump everything in the center like you're building a mozzarella sinkhole. That's a fast track to a soggy, underbaked middle. Instead, work from the outside in, taking care to spread your toppings evenly and take them all the way to the edges—especially the cheese. That border-hugging layer is what gives Detroit-style its signature crispy, cara-melized crust. No bare edges, no topping landslides, no sad center. Just balance, and lots of cheese, which, incidentally, is also my approach to wellness.

All this said, when it comes to pizza flavors, the only rule is to use what tastes good to you. As long as you're mindful of quantity, balance, and toppings distribution, it'll turn out well. If you love it, I love it.

To Parbake or Not to Parbake

If pizza were a religion, the crust would be its altar. In the case of Detroit-style pizza, with its frico edges and sturdy bottom, the crust is basically a golden, grease-kissed throne where cheese goes to ascend directly to heaven—amen and Shabbat Shalom. In other words, it's ***very*** important. Detroit-style pizza is already on the saucy, extra-cheesy side, and without a sturdy base, it can be like trying to eat lasagna with your hands (which, admittedly, isn't beneath me). There are a variety of ways to avoid this, and one of them is parbaking.

For the uninitiated, parbaking means partially baking your crust before layering on sauce and toppings. Think of it like giving your dough a pep talk before sending it into battle. It's not always necessary—but there are times when it can mean the difference between a crisp, chewy bottom and a sad, soggy sponge of regret. It's a requirement when you're making pies using my Gluten-Free Dough (page 41), which is far too batter-like when raw to build a pie on. Parbaking it makes it stable enough to top. But when you're using standard wheat-based pizza dough, it can be a little bit more of a judgment call.

So, when does it make sense to parbake? A few key situations. First, if you're working with a hefty load of toppings, such as the Ellen Supreme (page 85) or the Elote Pie (page 104), it helps your base stay proud and crisp—not limp and sorry for itself. Second, if your oven doesn't quite hit pizzeria temps and tends to melt cheese into oblivion before the bottom's even browned, a quick parbake gives your crust a fighting chance, even while baking below 500°F. It's also a smart move if you're prepping ahead—say, stocking the freezer for quick weeknight dinners or getting party pies ready to go. A parbaked crust is like a time-saving secret weapon: crisp, convenient, and ready when you are.

But exercise restraint and make sure you're just parbaking, not ***baking***-baking. If you overdo it, too much heat too early can dry your crust out before it ever gets the chance to achieve the signature chewy-light-interior-meets-crunchy-bottom. Detroit-style is ***meant*** to be baked as a whole—dough, cheese, toppings, one big, glorious mess—so if your oven runs hot, you're not drowning it in wet ingredients, and you're planning to build and eat your pizza within a fairly limited time frame, you can likely skip the parbake.

In short: Parbake with purpose. Like everything in life, there are times when it's warranted, and times when it isn't. For the times when it is, here's how to do it.

1. After your dough has proofed in the pan, preheat the oven to 550°F (or as high as it goes).

2. Bake for 7 to 9 minutes, just until the dough is firm and has begun to pull away from the edges of the pan. It should still be mostly pale and not be browned throughout.

3. Let it cool slightly. If you're planning to use the crust right away, take it out of the pan and let it cool on a rack—otherwise, the steam gets trapped and the bottom goes soft. If you're prepping ahead and want to keep a little moisture in the crumb (say, you're finishing the pie later that day or even

a few days out), let it cool in the pan. It'll stay a bit softer, which is actually helpful if you're not baking it again right away. To remove it, loosen the edges by running a thin metal spatula or butter knife gently along the edges of the crust to loosen any spots that may have stuck, especially the corners where cheese or oil might have caramelized.

4. Lift carefully: Slide a large offset spatula (or two, if needed) underneath the crust, starting at one end and working your way under. The bottom should be firm enough to lift in one piece.

5. Transfer to a cooling rack or work surface: Place the parbaked crust on a wire rack if you want to keep it crisp while it cools.

6. If you're topping it right away, no need to remove it. Just top and bake as desired. Since the base will have already gotten a head start, it likely won't need to bake as long as it would if you were starting with raw dough, so keep an eye on it. Once the cheese is browned and bubbly and the toppings are cooked through, it's done.

If you choose *not* to parbake, here's what to keep in mind about bake times, temperatures, and ovens:

The pies in this book were developed to be baked in a home oven at 550°F, parbaked or otherwise. For a fully topped Detroit-style pizza using 560 grams of raw dough in a 10-by-14-inch pan, bake for 15 to 18 minutes at 550°F, rotating the pan once if needed for even browning, then broil a little bit for extra browning, if desired. If your oven has a convection option, use it.

At 550°F, you're blasting it hot and fast—ideal for a crispy base, browned cheese edges, and cooked-through dough. For pies loaded with sauce, cheese, and toppings (especially heavier ones like bacon, sausage, or vegetables), you'll need that full 12- to 15-minute range.

If your oven goes up to only 475° or 500°F, you may need a bit longer—18 to 22 minutes.

No matter your oven, here are some checkpoints to keep in mind as your pie cooks:

1. At 10 minutes, peek at the cheese—it should be bubbling and browning.

2. By 12 to 13 minutes, the edges should be deeply golden and pulling away slightly from the pan.

3. At 15 minutes, the bottom should be crisp and dark golden brown—use a spatula to lift and check. If it isn't, continue baking for another 2 to 3 minutes, and continue the lift-and-check process until the pie is fully cooked with a crisp bottom.

DOUGH BASICS

Introduction

I realize this sounds kind of dramatic, but I'm not exaggerating when I tell you that pizza dough is a deeply emotional thing for me. By this I don't just mean that a perfectly cooked pie with a gorgeously open crumb and a shatteringly crisp, just barely charred undercarriage has the capacity to make me cry (though it absolutely does). What I'm saying—funny though it may sound—is that learning how to tune in to the sacred, time-honored process through which yeast particles awaken from deep sleep, then get to work turning a simple mixture of flour, water, and salt into soft, pliable dough that bakes into a bread product with a crisp exterior, lovely open texture with lots of air pockets, and a satisfying chew helped me understand myself in ways I didn't realize was possible.

Before I got into pizza, my feelings about cooking were fairly neutral. I could throw together an acceptable (if not particularly inspired) weeknight dinner, and I knew how to man a grill, but beyond that, I neither cared much about cooking nor was particularly skilled at it. When I started making pizza, everything changed. Not only was it fun to do and the results nice to eat, but it was also genuinely therapeutic. I fell in love with the way that occupying my hands and mind with the seemingly mindless tasks of mixing, kneading, and stretching dough helped me tune out the world—and everything within it that was stressing me out. With every batch of dough I made, not only did the pizzas I turned it into improve, but also the deep, meditative state I was able to get into quieted my mind and let me zero in on feelings I didn't know were there. It still happens, even all these years later. Whenever I need to figure something out, I get out the flour and let my mind do its thing.

You might think my big feelings about dough mean that I'm going to get all precious about the nuances of pizza dough and scream at you about using hand-ground heritage flours and checking your thermostat obsessively to ensure that your kitchen stays at exactly 72°F. Please. I would never. Not only because I'm actually a pretty nice guy, but also because I think most of the "rules" of dough-making are actually pretty fungible. There's no right or wrong. Dough is a living, breathing thing that operates on a bell curve and is more forgiving than you might think. Even if you don't execute every step perfectly, you're still pretty likely to get solid results, and although it takes some practice to get really good at dough, I'm living proof that it's achievable.

Here are a few things to keep in mind as you begin your dough journey:

If you haven't read my rant on using a scale, please turn to page 22, then come back here. Using a kitchen scale to measure your ingredients is far and away the number one thing that will help you level up your dough. It's easier than scooping and leveling, it'll help you achieve consistently good results, and, as a little bonus, it makes cleanup a snap because you only have to wash one bowl.

Once you mix your dough and see it begin to rise, treat it like someone you really like but have already texted three times. In other words, *leave it alone*. It's literally in the process of coming to life, and poking and prodding it will interfere and mess it up. Think of what you want in the first few moments of waking up in the morning—a nice warm bed, a calm environment, and nobody bugging you. Your dough wants the same thing, so trust the process, keep it covered, and let it do its thing. It'll let you know when it's ready.

Once your dough has visibly finished rising, be mindful of inadvertently degassing it by handling it too roughly. Keeping it full of air will lead to big, open pockets within the cooked dough, which is what we're looking for.

Use your senses. While the dough recipes in this book are time-tested, there are lots of little things that can influence how they work in your kitchen: the temperature of the room, the age of your yeast and flour, the kneading power of your hands or stand mixer. These factors impact how your dough looks, feels, rises, and bakes, so use your judgment. If your dough is nice and smooth by minute seven of kneading, then don't feel like you have to keep going for the 8 to 10 minutes the recipe calls for. If it hasn't quite doubled by the end of the prescribed rise time, give it a little longer.

No matter what, your dough is probably going to taste good after you top and bake it, so proceed with confidence, even if it might not be perfect. If you're new at this, chances are that you'll probably mess it up a little at first. Not only is this okay, but it's actually a good thing, because it means that with each batch, you'll internalize what works and what doesn't work, and after a while, that adds up to the excellent feeling of knowing what you're doing.

The doughs in this chapter are my favorites to work with, but feel free to experiment with any pizza dough you like. A general rule in Detroit-style pizza-making is that you want 4 to 5 grams of dough per square inch of pan. Since the pizza recipes in this book are for a 10-by-14-inch Detroit-style pizza pan, these dough recipes all yield between 600 and 700 grams of dough. If you're using a pan that's a different size, it's a good idea to weigh your dough before putting it in the pan to make sure you're in the right ballpark.

It's all about hydration. Understanding hydration (the ratio of water to flour in pizza dough) is crucial to making exceptional pizza, especially Detroit-style. Bakers use a simple system called "baker's percentages," where flour is always considered 100 percent, and every other ingredient is calculated as a percentage of that flour weight. To determine hydration, you just use this straightforward equation: **(water weight ÷ flour weight) × 100 = hydration percentage**. For example, if a dough recipe calls for 700 grams of flour and 490 grams of water, the hydration is (490 ÷ 700) × 100, or 70 percent.

Detroit-style pizza benefits from a relatively high-hydration dough, which results in a fluffy, tender interior and a crisp, airy crust with beautifully caramelized edges. This dough is a bit wetter and stickier than typical pizza dough. The extra moisture allows it to rise significantly in the pan, like focaccia, and it's what gives Detroit-style pizza its distinctive thick yet incredibly light texture.

Demystifying Fermentation

Alright, let's talk ***fermentation***—a word that sounds like it belongs in a lab coat but is actually more "lazy magic" than "science wizardry." When it comes to pizza dough, fermentation is the secret handshake between time and flour that unlocks that deep, complex flavor and airy-chewy texture that makes you feel like a dough sorcerer. And here's the wild part: You don't need to know jack about enzymes or yeast strains; you just need to learn to be patient while your yeast (whatever type you're using—more on that in a bit) does its thing. If you can clear some space in your fridge and not poke the dough every five minutes, congrats—you're halfway there.

So, let's break down the basics.

As you can probably infer from the names of my dough recipes, different kinds of dough need varying amounts of time to properly ferment—that is, for the flavor to develop and for the dough to rise, giving you a light, airy crust with just the right amount of chew. Even my simplest dough, made with yeast, flour, water, and salt, requires fermentation. It can be done in as little as a few hours, or you can do a longer rest in the fridge for more complex flavor.

You'll also find recipes that call for a slightly different approach to getting that classic rise. In some cases, flour and water are mixed and left to ferment before incorporating enough flour and water to make a full dough. ***Pre-ferment*** is the umbrella term here. It's like a little pre-party ***starter***. Each has its own vibe, but they all serve the same purpose: making your pizza crust chewier, crustier, and more "Damn, did I actually make this?"

Poolish, which you'll find in my Long Weekend Dough (page 38), is the French cool kid. It's a 1:1 mix of flour and water with a teeny bit of yeast. You mix it up, cover it, and leave it overnight. It'll get bubbly and smell slightly boozy, like it's been out drinking with a baguette. It adds a lightness and complex flavor to your dough without being fussy. Then there's biga, the Italian cousin—similar idea, but drier and stiffer, more like a dough than a batter. It ferments more slowly and gives your pizza a stronger, nuttier flavor and a chewier bite. If poolish is a sparkling wine spritz, biga is a neat glass of grappa—more serious, but still a good time.

Sourdough Starter (page 34) is the wild child of the bunch—literally. Unlike poolish and biga, which rely on commercial yeast, sourdough is 100 percent au naturel—just flour, water, and the wild yeast and bacteria floating around your kitchen. It takes longer to develop (we're talking days, not hours), and it requires a little upkeep (feeding it like a weird flour pet), but it gives your dough a deep, tangy flavor and a bit of funky complexity. But again—don't fear it. Once you've got a starter going, it's hard to kill. It's not unlike you and me—it just wants to live, eat, and make delicious carbs.

Bottom line: It may seem a little intimidating if you're new to baking, but fermentation doesn't have to be scary. Understanding the relationship between flour, yeast, and time is a lazy baker's secret weapon. You mix them up, leave them alone, and they do all the heavy lifting while you start daydreaming about pizza toppings. If you can wait, you can ferment. And if you mess up? It's dough. Worst case, you made weird bread, which, honestly, is probably still pretty tasty. Best case? You just leveled up your pizza game and can now drop words like ***poolish*** and ***starter*** into regular conversation like you've been doing it for years.

Slick Pans and Greasy Hands: Choosing a Fat for Your Pan

Choosing a fat to grease your Detroit-style pizza pan comes mostly down to function—and sometimes flavor gets a tiny little say too. Olive oil is my usual pick, which is why it's what is listed in the recipes in this book. This is partly because it tastes good and is the classic choice, but also, I use it in my doughs and I hate putting stuff away, so I let it do double duty. But olive oil's liquidity can make things tricky, especially for beginners, because dough tends to slide or retract annoyingly when you're stretching it out, leading to occasional frustration or complete and utter meltdowns. Solid fats, like butter or vegetable shortening, provide a sturdier grip, keeping your dough firmly in place and making the stretching job smoother and more manageable. Because let's face it—there's nothing worse than baking the perfect pie and being unable to get it out of the pan.

SAME-DAY DOUGH

This is my go-to, basic pizza dough recipe. It's relatively high in hydration, 70 percent (see page 30 for more about dough hydration), which helps form the tender, airy crumb Detroit-style pizza is famous for, but it's also great for any type of pizza (or any of the recipes in the Out of the Box chapter, page 128). I recommend using a stand mixer for this recipe if you've got one, mostly for ease of preparation, but you can definitely make it by hand, too.

YIELD: ONE 10-BY-14-INCH PIZZA CRUST

2¼ cups (320 g) bread flour, plus more for dusting

2 teaspoons (6 g) Diamond Crystal kosher salt (see salt conversion table on page 21 if using other salt)

1 teaspoon (3 g) instant yeast

1 cup (237 g) warm water

4 tablespoons (56 g) extra-virgin olive oil, divided, plus more for oiling hands

In the bowl of a stand mixer fitted with a dough hook attachment, on the lowest speed, stir to combine the flour, salt, and yeast.

Slowly stream in the water, then continue to mix for approximately 1 minute, or until shaggy.

Add 1 tablespoon (14 g) of the olive oil and mix for 30 seconds, or until the dough pulls away from the sides of the bowl. Increase the speed to medium and mix for an additional 1 to 2 minutes, or until smooth and elastic.

Let the dough rest in the bowl for 5 minutes.

Transfer the dough to a floured work surface and form into a ball. Lightly coat the dough and a mixing bowl with oil. Place the dough in the bowl, seam-side down. Tightly cover with plastic wrap and let rest for 20 minutes, just until the dough begins to expand.

Return the dough to the work surface and reshape it into a ball. Coat the ball with 1 tablespoon (14 g) of oil.

Use the remaining 2 tablespoons (28 g) of olive oil to grease a 10-by-14-inch Detroit pizza pan (or a similarly sized baking pan) and place the dough ball in the center. Use your hands to gently flatten the ball of dough. Don't worry about stretching it; you'll do that later, once it's relaxed.

Tightly cover the pan with plastic wrap. Let proof 2 hours, or until the dough has doubled in size.

With lightly oiled hands, push the dough to the edges of the pan.

Tightly re-cover the pan with plastic wrap or a fitted lid and refrigerate for at least 12 hours (or as long as 48—the longer it rests in the fridge, the more flavor the dough will have).

When ready to bake, remove the dough from the refrigerator and let it come to room temperature, 1 to 2 hours.

Top and bake as directed in each recipe for optimal results.

SOURDOUGH STARTER

Starting a sourdough starter can feel intimidating, but I promise you can do it. Like all pre-ferments, all it takes is a few simple ingredients—in this case water and bread flour—and a bit of patience. This starter recipe uses equal parts bread flour and filtered water, making it easy to manage and perfect for beginners. Keep in mind that consistency is key—feed your starter regularly, and don't be discouraged by slow beginnings. For best results, let your starter ferment somewhere slightly warm, like your oven with just the oven light on, creating an ideal cozy environment. While this starter is featured here for Detroit-style pizza dough, you'll quickly discover it's versatile enough for all yeast-leavened baked goods.

YIELD: 200 GRAMS OF SOURDOUGH STARTER

⅔ cup (100 g) bread flour

⅓ cup plus 1½ tablespoons (100 g) filtered water, at room temperature

NOTE: WHILE YOU *CAN* USE A MEASURING CUP FOR THE FLOUR AND WATER, AS ALWAYS, I HIGHLY RECOMMEND YOU USE A SCALE AND MEASURE IN GRAMS.

Day 1: Mix 100 grams of bread flour with 100 grams of filtered water in a glass jar or bowl until thoroughly combined and no dry flour remains. Cover loosely with a cloth or plastic wrap and place it in your oven with the oven light turned on to create gentle warmth.

Day 2: Discard half of your starter, leaving approximately 100 grams behind. Feed it another 100 grams each of bread flour and filtered water, stirring well. Cover again loosely and return it to the warm oven environment.

Days 3 to 7: Repeat the discard-and-feed process each day. You should see bubbles and notice a slightly tangy smell developing—this means your starter is becoming active!

By day 7, your starter should double in size within 4 to 8 hours of feeding, indicating it's ready to use.

TIPS

- Regular feeding keeps your starter healthy.
- If your starter forms liquid on top (known as "hooch"), just stir it in—it's normal.
- Keep the starter at room temperature for frequent baking or refrigerate and feed weekly if using less often.

SOUR FRANCISCO

2-DAY DOUGH

This dough takes longer to be ready than the Same-Day Dough but requires far less hands-on effort, developing mostly during its extended fridge rest. It's ideal when you plan to make pizza within a few days but don't have the time or energy to actively manage the dough. The long, cold fermentation results in a deeply flavorful dough with an open crumb. Beyond pizza, it works beautifully as focaccia (page 132) or even shaped into a loaf pan for easy sandwich bread, making it exceptionally versatile and convenient.

YIELD: ONE 10-BY-14-INCH PIZZA CRUST

2¼ cups (320 g) bread flour, plus more for dusting

2 teaspoons (6 g) Diamond Crystal kosher salt (see the salt conversion table on page 21 if using other salt)

1 teaspoon (3 g) instant yeast

1 cup (237 g) water, at room temperature

3 tablespoons (42 g) extra-virgin olive oil, divided, plus more for coating the dough

Combine the flour, salt, yeast, water, and 1 tablespoon (14 g) of the olive oil in a large mixing bowl.

Mix with hands or a wooden spoon until no dry flour remains.

Cover the bowl and let it rest for 5 minutes.

Uncover the bowl and place a bowl scraper or your hand (wet it or coat with a bit of flour to prevent sticking) between the side of the bowl and the dough, then stretch the bottom of the dough up and over its top, as if folding it in half. Repeat this process three more times, turning the bowl 90 degrees each time, until you've turned it completely around.

Cover the bowl and let rest for 15 minutes, then repeat the folding process.

Repeat the resting/folding cycle twice more for a total of four times.

Cover the bowl tightly with plastic wrap or a fitted lid, then refrigerate for 18 to 24 hours. The dough should double in size.

Use the remaining 2 tablespoons (28 g) of olive oil to grease a 10-by-14-inch Detroit-style pizza pan (or similar-sized pan).

Gently deflate the dough using two forks, a dough scraper, or a silicone scraper and transfer to a floured work surface.

Working quickly and carefully, form the dough into a ball and coat the dough liberally with olive oil.

Place the dough in the center of the greased pan and cover with plastic wrap.

Let the dough rest in the center of the pan for 20 to 30 minutes, until it has relaxed and become pliable.

Use your hands to gently press the dough into the base of the pan in an even layer, ensuring that it stretches to all four corners.

Cover the pan and let it rest at room temperature for another 2 hours, or until the dough rises to about twice its height. Alternately, cover the pan with plastic wrap or a fitted lid and let rise in the refrigerator for up to 48 hours, then let rest at room temperature for 1 to 2 hours.

Top and bake as directed in each recipe for optimal results.

LONG WEEKEND DOUGH

This dough takes a bit of planning, but it delivers extraordinary flavor, a crunchy exterior, and a beautifully bubbly interior. The secret is a pre-ferment called poolish (see page 30 for more about pre-ferments). Mixing a small amount of yeast with flour and water beforehand enhances both rise and flavor, adding a deliciously tangy, almost sourdough-like depth. Perfect for leisurely weekends at home—or any time you're around to manage the simple steps. Semolina adds a nutty richness, but if you prefer, swap it out for an extra ⅓ cup (40 g) of bread flour.

YIELD: ONE 10-BY-14-INCH PIZZA CRUST

PRE-FERMENT (POOLISH)

Pinch of instant yeast

⅔ cup (158 g) cold water

1 cup plus 3 tablespoons (158 g) bread flour

DOUGH

⅓ cup plus 1 tablespoon (87 g) warm water

3 tablespoons (42 g) extra-virgin olive oil, divided, plus more for oiling hands

1 cup plus 1 tablespoon (142 g) bread flour

¼ cup plus 1 tablespoon (50 g) semolina

2¼ teaspoons (7 g) Diamond Crystal kosher salt (see the salt conversion table on page 21 if using other salt)

Heaping ¼ teaspoon (1 g) instant yeast

TO MAKE THE POOLISH

Sprinkle the yeast over the cold water in a medium bowl. Add the flour and mix with a wooden spoon until completely combined. Cover with plastic wrap or a fitted lid and leave in a draft-free place (like a turned-off microwave or oven with the door shut) for 18 to 24 hours. The poolish should triple in size and become very bubbly.

TO MAKE THE DOUGH

Add the warm water and 1 tablespoon (14 g) of the extra-virgin olive oil to the poolish and stir well with a wooden spoon to break it up.

Combine the bread flour, semolina, salt, and yeast in a large mixing bowl and whisk to combine.

Add the poolish-water-oil mixture to the dry ingredients and mix until a shaggy dough forms.

Knead the dough for 1 minute, just until it can be shaped into a ball.

Cover the bowl with plastic wrap or a fitted lid and let rest in a warm place for 2 hours. It should double in size.

Using floured hands on a floured surface or a stand mixer fitted with a dough hook, knead the dough (on medium speed if using the mixer) for 8 to 10 minutes, until it's very smooth and elastic.

Coat the dough with 1 tablespoon (14 g) of olive oil and return it to the bowl. Cover and let rise in the refrigerator for 48 hours. The dough should at least double in size.

Use the remaining 1 tablespoon (14 g) of olive oil to grease a 10-by-14-inch Detroit-style pizza pan (or another metal pan of similar size). Place the risen dough in the center of the greased pan and cover with plastic wrap. Let rest for 50 minutes to 1 hour until very soft and pliable.

Once the dough has rested and is very pliable, use your hands to gently press the dough into the base of the pan in an even layer, ensuring that it stretches to all four corners.

Tightly cover the pan with plastic wrap. Let proof for 50 minutes to 1 hour, or until the dough has doubled in size.

With lightly oiled hands, push the dough to the edges of the pan.

Tightly re-cover the pan with plastic wrap and refrigerate for at least 8 hours (or as long as 48—the longer it rests in the fridge, the more flavor the dough will have).

When ready to bake, remove the dough from the refrigerator and let it come to room temperature, 1 to 2 hours.

Top and bake as directed in each recipe for optimal results.

GLUTEN-FREE DOUGH

I eat plenty of gluten, but I'm still extremely proud of this recipe, because great pizza should be for everyone, no matter your dietary restrictions. After extensive trials, we developed a gluten-free dough so tasty that customers frequently insist it must contain gluten. My gluten-intolerant wife, Tess, loves it, which is all the proof I need that it's truly excellent. While any 1:1 gluten-free flour will work, Cup4Cup, created by Chef Thomas Keller, yields unmatched texture and chew. The dough behaves more like a thick batter, rising less than wheat-based doughs, yet baking into a sturdy, crispy-bottomed crust with an airy crumb—perfectly suited for Detroit-style toppings.

YIELD: ONE 10-BY-14-INCH PIZZA CRUST

3¼ cups (382 g) 1:1 gluten-free flour (Cup4Cup strongly recommended)

1⅓ cups plus 1 tablespoon (335 g) warm water

2¼ teaspoons (7 g) instant yeast

2 teaspoons (6 g) Diamond Crystal kosher salt (see the salt conversion table on page 21 if using other salt)

3 tablespoons (42 g) extra-virgin olive oil, divided

In a large bowl or stand mixer, combine the gluten-free flour, warm water, and yeast.

Stir constantly or mix on low for 5 minutes. The dough will look more like a batter, so don't worry if it seems wet.

Add the salt and 1 tablespoon (14 g) of the olive oil.

Stir constantly or mix on low for 10 minutes. The dough will still be quite wet but will thicken slightly and be very smooth.

Cover the bowl and allow the dough to proof in a warm spot for 1½ hours. It may not double completely, but it should expand.

Coat a 10-by-14-inch Detroit-style pizza pan with the remaining 2 tablespoons (28 g) of olive oil and scrape the dough into the pan.

Cover with plastic wrap or a fitted lid and allow the dough to proof in the pan for 1½ to 2 hours, or overnight in the fridge.

Preheat the oven to 550°F (or as hot as your oven allows) for at least an hour.

Parbake the crust for 5 to 7 minutes, until firm and lightly browned.

Remove the parbaked dough from the oven and top as desired, then return to the oven for an additional 13 to 15 minutes to finish cooking.

Discard Recipe Ideas

Sourdough discard isn't waste—it's flavor ready to happen. Sure, you can toss your discard, but why not turn it into a bonus dish? It can transform everyday dishes, adding subtle tang and depth—plus, since it's basically already batter, you often only need to add a few ingredients to give it new life. Here are six quick and easy ways to put your discard to delicious use.

SOURDOUGH CRACKERS

Mix 100 grams of sourdough discard with 2 tablespoons (28 g) extra-virgin olive oil, ½ teaspoon (1.5 g) Diamond Crystal kosher salt (see the salt conversion table on page 21 if using other salt), and 1 teaspoon (1 to 1.5 g) finely chopped fresh herbs of your choice. Roll very thin, cut into shapes, and bake at 350°F until crisp and golden, about 20 to 25 minutes.

DISCARD PANCAKES

Whisk 100 grams of starter with 1 egg, ½ cup (125 g) milk of your choice, ½ cup (60 g) all-purpose flour, and 1 teaspoon (4 g) baking powder. Ladle onto a lightly greased skillet over medium heat and cook until bubbles form and the edges begin to dry. Flip and cook just until golden on the other side, then serve with butter, syrup, fruit, or your favorite jam.

SOURDOUGH FLATBREAD

Stir together 100 grams of discard, ½ cup (60 g) all-purpose flour, 1 tablespoon (14 g) extra-virgin olive oil, and a generous pinch of salt. Knead just until smooth, then divide into four pieces. Roll into rounds (they don't need to be perfect) and cook in a dry skillet over medium-high heat for 1 to 2 minutes per side, until puffed and browned. Serve warm with your favorite soup, salad, curry, or dip.

QUICK SCALLION PANCAKES

Stir together 100 grams of starter with ¼ cup (30 g) all-purpose flour, ¼ cup (about 25 g) finely chopped scallions, and a pinch of salt. Pour into a hot, generously oiled skillet over medium-high heat and cook until crispy and brown on both sides.

SOURDOUGH WAFFLES

Whisk together 100 grams of discard with ¾ cup (90 g) all-purpose flour, 1 tablespoon (12.5 g) granulated sugar, 1 teaspoon (4 g) baking powder, ½ teaspoon (1.5 g) Diamond Crystal kosher salt (see the salt conversion table on page 21 if using other salt), 1 egg, ¾ cup (183 g) whole milk, and 2 tablespoons (28 g) melted butter. Cook in a lightly greased waffle iron until golden and crisp.

QUICK PAN PIZZA

Mix 100 grams of sourdough discard with ½ cup (60 g) all-purpose or bread flour, ⅓ cup (about 80 g) warm water, 1 tablespoon (14 g) olive oil, and ¼ teaspoon (0.7 g) Diamond Crystal kosher salt (see the salt conversion table on page 21 if using other salt) until sticky. Spread into an oiled 8-inch skillet or baking pan, let rest for 30 minutes, then top and bake at 450° F for 15 to 20 minutes, or until puffed and golden.

STAYCATION SOURDOUGH

Unlike the Long Weekend Dough, which just asks you to commit to a couple of days and a poolish, this one assumes you're already in a relationship—with your sourdough starter. (See page 34 for guidance on starting and maintaining a sourdough starter.) It's the kind of dough you make when you've got time to hang out at home, feed your starter, and check in on your dough between other cozy stay-at-home activities. The flavor is complex and tangy, the texture is chewy with a crisp bottom, and the whole process feels a little like a love letter to slow living.

YIELD: ONE 10-BY-14-INCH PIZZA CRUST

¼ cup (50 g) active, bubbly sourdough starter

¾ cup (205 g) water, at room temperature

2⅜ cups (302 g) bread flour

2 teaspoons (6 g) Diamond Crystal kosher salt (see the salt conversion table on page 21 if using other salt)

3 tablespoons (42 g) extra-virgin olive oil, divided, plus more for oiling hands

In a large mixing bowl, combine the sourdough starter and water to dissolve. Add the flour and salt. Mix until no dry bits remain. The dough will be shaggy and sticky—this is normal.

Let the dough rest for 30 to 45 minutes. This helps the flour hydrate fully and kick-starts gluten development.

Mix 1 tablespoon (14 g) of the olive oil into the dough by hand. Then begin the stretch and folds: Grab one edge, stretch it up, and fold over itself. Rotate the bowl and repeat three or four times. Cover the bowl and let rest for 30 minutes. Repeat two or three more times over the next 90 minutes. The rested dough should be supple and taut to the touch.

Cover the bowl and let it ferment at room temperature, ideally 70° to 75°F, for 4 to 6 hours, or until the dough has roughly doubled in size.

Use the remaining 2 tablespoons (28 g) of olive oil to grease a 10-by-14-inch Detroit-style pizza pan (or another metal pan of similar size). Place the risen dough in the center and cover with plastic wrap. Let rest for 50 minutes to 1 hour until very soft and pliable.

Once the dough has rested and is very pliable, gently press it into an even layer, ensuring that it stretches to all four corners.

Tightly cover the pan. Proof for 50 minutes to 1 hour, or until doubled in size.

With lightly oiled hands, push the dough to the edges of the pan.

Tightly cover the pan and refrigerate for at least 12 hours.

When ready to bake, remove the dough from the refrigerator and let it come to room temperature, 1 to 2 hours.

Top and bake as directed in each recipe for optimal results.

GET SAUCED

Introduction

In the world of Detroit-style pizza, the classic "upside-down pie" is often treated like sacred geometry—a bright stripe of cooked tomato sauce ladled on post-bake, meant to cut through the richness of the bubbling cheese and frico-crisped edges. When done with restraint, it can be a beautiful thing, but when the sauce is applied with too heavy a hand, suddenly the pie becomes more marinara delivery system than pizza. That's where a lighter hand and a little imagination comes in.

My perspective is that this rule, like all rules, is made to be loosened, if not broken. I view the upside-down pie a starting point rather than gospel. Enter: a new era of toppings that balance the old-school charm with modern swagger. Think creamy, chile-spiked ranch drizzled over pepperoni, or a swipe of garlicky cream sauce hidden under the cheese, topped with a post-bake flourish of chile crisp or pesto. These touches do more than just look pretty for the camera; they're a reminder that pizza, like any genre, thrives on remixing.

Barbecue sauce brings a smoky-sweet bass note that sings alongside caramelized onions or pulled pork. And hot honey? At this point, it's less of a trend and more of requirement, transforming sausage or crispy edges into caramelized, sticky perfection, and I wouldn't have it any other way.

The best pies often lean into contrast: cooked sauces layered under bubbling cheese for depth, with bright, fresh drizzles, herbs, and uncooked Parm or Grana Padano on top for zing and pop. Don't get me wrong: An upside-down pie can still play its part! But I think sharing the stage with other sauces and finishers makes for a more dynamic, craveable bite.

In this chapter, you'll find a mix of classics and wild cards to keep your pies interesting. The Red Sauce (page 46) is as stripped-down as it gets—just tomatoes with a kiss of oregano, no sugar, no fuss. House Ranch (page 64) is made from scratch and makes the bottled stuff taste like regret. Fresh Herb Pesto (page 61) adds a blast of brightness and works on everything from white pies to veggie-forward ones. SPG BBQ Sauce (page 69) brings smoky heat and sweetness—great with pork or roasted mushrooms. The White Sauce (page 50) is the opposite of heavy—made with cream, garlic, lemon, and ricotta, it's fresh and tangy, not gloopy or cloying. And the creamy Vodka Sauce (page 49), spiked with Calabrian peppers, walks that perfect line between comfort and heat. Some of these are paired with specific pies, but they're all versatile enough to sneak into your own signature combos.

RED SAUCE

This is the sauce that started it all, and the one we use the most at the restaurant. It's uncooked, unfussy, and unapologetically tomato-forward, with just enough tang. The oregano gives it just a whisper of pizza parlor nostalgia, and the no-cook method keeps the tomato flavor bright and clean. Whether it's layered under cheese or used as a post-bake red top, this sauce does its job without stealing the show.

YIELD: ABOUT 3½ CUPS

One 28-ounce (784 g) can crushed San Marzano tomatoes

1 teaspoon (3 g) kosher salt (see the salt conversion table on page 21 if using other salt)

½ teaspoon (0.5 g) dried oregano

Place all the ingredients in a medium mixing bowl and stir well to combine.

Cover the bowl or transfer the sauce to an airtight container and refrigerate until ready to use.

NOTE: DON'T LET ANYONE TELL YOU THAT THE ONLY GOOD TOMATOES COME FROM EUROPE. I LIVE IN CALIFORNIA, AND SOME OF THE BEST TOMATOES I'VE EVER HAD WERE GROWN HERE. JUST USE TOMATOES THAT TASTE GOOD TO YOU.

VODKA SAUCE

VODKA SAUCE

Vodka sauce on pizza has gained popularity over the past few years, but it's been number one in my heart for a long, long time. The vodka's sharp flavor and alcohol content cook away, but the booze helps emulsify the tomatoes and cream into a silky, luxurious texture while enhancing the tomato's natural sweetness. If you want to make an alcohol-free version, just use water to deglaze the pan—it'll work nearly as well. This sauce is perfectly suited for sausage pies, dollops of ricotta, or even a simple mozzarella-topped slice.

YIELD: ABOUT 1½ CUPS

2 tablespoons (28 g) extra-virgin olive oil

2 cloves garlic (about 6 g), chopped

1 medium yellow onion, chopped (about 1 cup / 150 g)

1 tablespoon (15 g) Calabrian chile paste or 1 teaspoon crushed red chile flakes

½ teaspoon (1.5 g) Diamond Crystal kosher salt (see the salt conversion table on page 21 if using other salt)

Pinch of crushed red chile flakes

2 tablespoons (33 g) tomato paste

¼ cup (60 g) vodka

1 cup (240 g) crushed tomatoes

⅔ cup (150 g) heavy cream

A few drops red wine vinegar

Heat the olive oil in a medium saucepan over medium heat. Add the garlic and onion and cook, stirring occasionally, until softened and lightly golden, 5 to 7 minutes.

Stir in the Calabrian chile paste, salt, crushed red chile flakes, and tomato paste. Cook for 2 minutes, stirring frequently, until the tomato paste deepens in color.

Pour in the vodka and let it simmer for about 2 minutes to cook off the alcohol, stirring to deglaze the pan. Add the crushed tomatoes and bring to a gentle simmer. Cook for 10 minutes, stirring occasionally, until thickened slightly.

Reduce the heat to low and stir in the heavy cream. Simmer for another 2 to 3 minutes, then finish with a few drops of red wine vinegar to brighten it up.

Let cool slightly before using. Store any extra in the fridge for up to 5 days.

WHITE SAUCE

Unlike the usual heavy, gloopy Alfredo-style sauces you might expect, this sauce is damn near lively. A hefty addition of lemon balances the creaminess, and the whole thing comes together in a mixing bowl—no cooking required. It's excellent as a base for veggie-forward pies, white clam pizza, or anything garlicky and herbaceous, but it can also play the part of bechamel in lasagnas beautifully.

YIELD: ABOUT 1½ CUPS

1 cup (233 g) whole-milk ricotta cheese

⅔ cup (160 g) heavy cream

1 teaspoon (3 g) Diamond Crystal kosher salt (see the salt conversion table on page 21 if using other salt)

½ teaspoon (about 1 g) freshly ground black pepper

2 cloves garlic (about 6 g), finely chopped

⅓ cup (113 g) lemon juice (about 1 large lemon or 1½ medium lemons)

In a medium bowl, combine the ricotta, heavy cream, salt, pepper, garlic, and lemon juice.

Whisk until smooth and creamy. Taste and adjust the seasoning if needed—the lemon should brighten the mix, but not overwhelm it.

Use immediately or store in an airtight container in the refrigerator for up to a week.

NOTE: THE FLAVOR OF THE RICOTTA REALLY SHINES THROUGH HERE, SO BUY THE BEST ONE YOU CAN FIND—PREFERABLY ONE MADE WITHOUT GUMS OR STABILIZERS.

ORGANIC
WHOLE
BLACK
PEPPERCORNS
MORTON & BASSETT SPICES
M B
SPICES
SAN FRANCISCO
NON-IRRADIATED
2 OZ ◆ 56g

BEET CREAM

BEET CREAM

This vibrant, earthy sauce gets its vivid color from pureed beets and its creamy body from sunflower seeds and garlic. The result is surprisingly balanced given its bright purple hue—sweet, nutty, tangy, and perfect on white pies (like the Beet-an-esca, page 92), spooned over grilled bread, drizzled on roasted carrots or potatoes for a colorful side dish, or tossed with nutty whole-wheat pasta.

YIELD: ABOUT 2 CUPS

1 pound (450 g) red beets, peeled and diced into 1-inch pieces

1 cup (130 g) shelled roasted, salted sunflower seeds

½ cup (110 g) extra-virgin olive oil

1 clove garlic (about 3 g), chopped

2 teaspoons (10 g) Garlic Confit cloves (page 60), drained, or 1 additional fresh garlic clove, chopped

¾ cup (180 g) fresh lemon juice

1½ teaspoons (4.5 g) Diamond Crystal kosher salt (see the salt conversion table on page 21 if using other salt)

1 teaspoon (2 g) freshly ground black pepper

Bring a large pot of water to a boil. Add the diced beets and cook until very tender, 20 to 25 minutes. Drain and let cool slightly. (If you prefer, you can instead roast the beets at 400°F for 40 to 45 minutes, or until very tender.)

In a food processor, add the sunflower seeds. Blend on low, then increase to high speed until finely ground, about 3 minutes. With the motor running, slowly drizzle in the olive oil. Blend for 2 more minutes, scraping down the sides as needed, until smooth.

Add the cooked beets to the sunflower mixture and blend until the beets are mostly broken down. Add the chopped garlic, Garlic Confit, lemon juice, salt, and pepper. Blend on high for 4 to 5 minutes, scraping down the sides as needed, until smooth and creamy.

Let the sauce cool to room temperature. Transfer to an airtight container and refrigerate for up to 5 days.

SUN-DRIED TOMATO VINAIGRETTE

This rich, tangy, umami-packed sauce gets its deep flavor from sun-dried tomatoes, slow-cooked garlic, and sautéed onions. It's perfect for drizzling over a cooked pizza, like the Veggie Pie Guy on page 121, on hot or cold roasted vegetables, or as the dressing for a light, summery pasta salad.

YIELD: ABOUT 1½ CUPS

ONIONS

1 tablespoon (14 g) extra-virgin olive oil

1 medium onion (122 g), chopped

¼ teaspoon (0.7 g) Diamond Crystal kosher salt (see the salt conversion table on page 21 if using other salt)

VINAIGRETTE

½ cup (80 g) sun-dried tomatoes

1 cup (240 g) hot water (not boiling—about 170°F)

¼ cup (40 g) Garlic Confit cloves (page 60), drained

¼ cup (60 g) red wine vinegar

½ teaspoon (1.5 g) Diamond Crystal kosher salt (see the salt conversion table on page 21 if using other salt)

½ teaspoon (1 g) freshly ground black pepper

⅓ cup (72 g) extra-virgin olive oil

TO PREPARE THE ONIONS

Heat a heavy-bottomed skillet over medium heat. Add the olive oil and onion.

Cook for 5 to 7 minutes, stirring occasionally, until golden brown. Sprinkle the salt over the cooked onions and stir to incorporate.

Transfer the onions to a bowl and set aside.

TO MAKE THE VINAIGRETTE

Place the sun-dried tomatoes in a small bowl and pour the hot water over them. Let them soak for 15 to 20 minutes, until softened.

In a blender or food processor, combine the soaked sun-dried tomatoes (along with their soaking liquid), Garlic Confit, cooked onions, red wine vinegar, salt, and pepper. Blend until mostly smooth, stopping to scrape down the sides as needed.

With the motor running, slowly drizzle in the olive oil and continue blending until the sauce is emulsified and creamy. Taste and adjust the seasoning if needed.

Transfer to a container and use immediately or refrigerate for up to 1 week.

SPG SALSA VERDE

This bright, flavorful sauce is packed with fresh dill and parsley, capers, garlic, and just enough acidity and spice to keep things interesting. It's the perfect balance to the earthy beets on the Beet-an-esca pie (page 92) or anything else that needs a pop of green freshness. I also love to use it as a drizzle for pizza, steak, roasted vegetables, or anything grilled.

YIELD: ABOUT ¾ CUP

⅔ cup (10 g) loosely packed fresh dill leaves (from 2 to 3 sprigs)

1 cup (15 g) loosely packed fresh Italian parsley leaves (from 4 to 5 sprigs)

⅓ cup (72 g) extra-virgin olive oil, plus more as needed

1 tablespoon (8 g) chopped garlic (about 1 large clove)

1 tablespoon (10 g) drained capers

¾ teaspoon (2.5 g) Diamond Crystal kosher salt (see the salt conversion table on page 21 if using other salt)

¾ teaspoon (2 g) freshly ground black pepper

1½ teaspoons (1.5 g) crushed red chile flakes

3 tablespoons (45 g) red wine vinegar

In a food processor, combine half the herbs with half the olive oil. Pulse until finely chopped, scraping down the sides as needed.

Add the remaining herbs and oil. Blend again until finely chopped and cohesive.

Add the garlic, capers, salt, pepper, crushed red chile flakes, and vinegar. Blend until smooth and sauce-like, scraping down the bowl as needed. If the texture is too chunky, blend in 15- to 30-second bursts, adding a touch more oil if desired.

Transfer to a clean jar and refrigerate. Use within 5 days.

KIJANI KIBICHI GREEN SAUCE

Named with a nod to the Swahili words for "lush green," this herby sauce, which came to Square Pie Guys courtesy of Chefs Solomon Johnson and Mike Woods of The Bussdown in Oakland when we collaborated on our Yardbird pie (page 99), is sweet, spicy, and citrusy, with a subtle tropical twist, courtesy of a little touch of pineapple juice. Think of it as chimichurri's more daring cousin—ideal for drizzling over roasted veg, serving with grilled meats, or swiping across the top of a pizza for a pop of freshness.

YIELD: ABOUT 2 CUPS

1 small bunch fresh cilantro, stems included (about 200 g)

3 tablespoons (45 g) fresh lemon juice

3 tablespoons (60 g) Hot Honey (page 67), or use store-bought, or combine regular honey and 1 teaspoon crushed red chile flakes

2 tablespoons (30 g) pineapple juice

½ teaspoon (2 g) minced fresh ginger

¼ teaspoon (0.5 g) cayenne pepper, or to taste

½ teaspoon (1.5 g) Diamond Crystal kosher salt (see the salt conversion table on page 21 if using other salt)

¼ teaspoon (0.7 g) freshly ground black pepper

½ cup (110 g) extra-virgin olive oil

In a blender or using an immersion blender, combine the cilantro, lemon juice, Hot Honey, pineapple juice, ginger, cayenne, salt, and pepper. Blend on low speed, gradually increasing to high, until finely chopped and well combined, 1 to 1½ minutes.

Add half the olive oil and blend for 30 seconds. Add the remaining oil and blend again until smooth and emulsified.

Taste and adjust the seasoning if needed. Transfer to a clean jar or bottle. Store in the refrigerator and use within 5 to 7 days. Shake well before each use.

KIJANI KIBICHI
GREEN SAUCE

TOMATO CONFIT

This confit is adapted from the one in Samin Nosrat's *Salt Fat Acid Heat*, and it also makes an appearance on the Summer Tomato Pie (page 103), which we developed with her. It's the perfect recipe to make at the peak of tomato season to really capture the sweetness of cherry tomatoes (especially super-sweet Sungolds, if you can find them), but I also love to make it in the dead of winter, with whatever tomatoes I can get my hands on, because even the mealiest supermarket tomatoes transform into pure sunshine after a long, olive oil bath in the oven.

YIELD: ABOUT 1½ CUPS

3½ cups (about 550 g) whole cherry or grape tomatoes

3 cloves garlic, peeled

3 or 4 large basil leaves (leave the stems attached)

½ cup (110 g) extra-virgin olive oil

½ teaspoon (1.5 g) Diamond Crystal kosher salt (see the salt conversion table on page 21 if using other salt)

Preheat the oven to 300°F.

Lay the cherry or grape tomatoes, garlic cloves, and basil in a single layer in a small roasting dish or oven-safe frying pan.

Cover with the olive oil. The tomatoes don't need to be completely submerged, but they should all have some contact with the olive oil.

Season with the salt and bake for 35 to 40 minutes, until the skins begin to split when pierced with a skewer or paring knife.

Let cool to room temperature. Store in an airtight container in the refrigerator for up to 2 weeks.

GARLIC CONFIT

Garlic confit is one of those kitchen gems that instantly upgrades everything it touches. Slow-cooked in olive oil until buttery-soft and mellow, the garlic loses its harsh bite and becomes rich, sweet, and spreadable. Use the cloves on pizza, in sauces, or smashed into toast. The infused oil is liquid gold—perfect for drizzling over finished pies or whisking into dressings. At the restaurant, we use garlic confit as the base for several dressings. It's the kind of thing you'll always want to have on hand.

YIELD: ABOUT 1 CUP

2 cups (about 300 g) garlic cloves, peeled

1 cup (220 g) extra-virgin olive oil

Add the garlic cloves and olive oil to a small saucepan. Set over the lowest heat possible and cook, uncovered, until the garlic is soft and pale golden, 45 to 60 minutes. The oil should gently bubble but never boil—if it starts to sizzle, reduce the heat.

Once the garlic is tender and jammy, remove from the heat and let cool to room temperature.

Transfer the cloves and oil to a clean jar or airtight container. Store in the refrigerator for up to 2 weeks. Always use a clean utensil when scooping to keep it fresh.

NOTE: FOR FOOD SAFETY, GARLIC CONFIT MUST BE KEPT REFRIGERATED. DO NOT STORE AT ROOM TEMPERATURE.

FRESH HERB PESTO

Herby and aromatic with a savory cheese backbone, this pesto is endlessly versatile. You'll notice it differs from traditional basil pesto in two ways. First, in addition to the usual fresh basil, it contains parsley and scallion tops. The result is a fresher-tasting, less floral pesto. The second notable difference from classic pesto is that it's made without pine nuts, which makes it lighter and easier to spoon over the top of a pie (or pasta, or grilled fish—it's good on just about anything!). If you wish, add ⅓ cup toasted pine nuts, walnuts, or blanched almonds to the blender with the garlic and cheese.

YIELD: ABOUT 1½ CUPS

2 cups (40 g) basil leaves, loosely packed

1 cup (20 g) flat-leaf parsley leaves, loosely packed

½ cup (25 g) scallion tops

1 or 2 cloves garlic, peeled and roughly chopped (3 to 6 g)

½ cup (45 g) grated Grana Padano or Parmesan

½ teaspoon (3 g) Diamond Crystal kosher salt, or to taste (see the salt conversion table on page 21 if using other salt)

¾ cup (165 g) extra-virgin olive oil

Roughly chop the herbs to aid blending.

In a blender or food processor, combine basil, parsley, scallion tops, garlic, cheese, salt, and olive oil.

Pulse for 30 seconds to a minute, until mostly smooth and bright green. Scrape down the sides as needed.

Transfer to a clean, airtight container. Store in the fridge for up to 1 week. Or, for long-term storage, freeze in ice cube trays, then remove the cubes and store them in a zip-top bag in the freezer for up to 3 months.

GREEN GODDESS CAESAR

This bright, punchy hybrid of Caesar and Green Goddess is a favorite at Square Pie Guys. It pulls in sharp garlic, lemon, and anchovy for depth, with heaps of fresh herbs for color and freshness. Use it as a pizza drizzle, salad dressing, sandwich spread, or veggie dip.

YIELD: ABOUT 2 CUPS

¾ cup (20 g) fresh Italian parsley leaves, loosely packed (a few tender stems are okay)

½ cup (15 g) fresh basil leaves, loosely packed (stems removed)

2 cloves garlic (about 6 g), roughly chopped

2 teaspoons(8 g) anchovy paste, or chopped anchovies packed in oil

1 teaspoon (2 g) freshly ground black pepper

½ teaspoon (1.5 g) Diamond Crystal kosher salt (see the salt conversion table on page 21 if using other salt)

¼ cup (25 g) grated Grana Padano or Parmesan

¼ cup (60 g) fresh lemon juice (from 1 or 2 large lemons)

¾ cup (180 g) mayonnaise

¼ cup (55 g) extra-virgin olive oil

Strip the parsley and basil leaves from their stems (a few small stems are fine, but avoid thick or woody ones).

In a blender or food processor, combine the garlic, anchovy paste, black pepper, salt, cheese, parsley, basil, and lemon juice. Blend until the herbs are very finely chopped and the mixture is thick. Scrape down the sides as needed.

Add the mayonnaise and olive oil. Blend again until creamy and emulsified, 30 to 60 seconds. Taste and adjust the seasoning if needed.

Transfer to a jar or container and refrigerate for up to a week. Stir well before using.

GREEN GODDESS CAESAR

HOUSE RANCH

This is ranch dressing the way it's meant to be—creamy, herb-packed, and a world away from anything that comes in a bottle. A blend of mayo, sour cream, and just enough buttermilk gives it a perfect balance of richness and tang, while fresh herbs, garlic, and a touch of Dijon make it bright and complex. It's an ideal dip for crusts, a cool drizzle on spicy pies, or a dressing for crisp greens if you somehow have leftovers. I like to make it by hand for an extra-chunky ranch with distinctive green/white contrasting, but if you prefer a smoother, greener ranch, feel free to use a blender or food processor.

We play with this one a lot at the restaurant. We'll blend in Calabrian chiles to make spicy ranch or vinegar-based hot sauce for Buffalo ranch. You can even throw in a few cloves of Garlic Confit (page 60) for a tangy, just barely sweet homage to the bulb that makes everything better.

YIELD: ABOUT 1¼ CUPS

½ cup (120 g) mayonnaise

½ cup (120 g) full-fat sour cream or Greek yogurt

¼ cup (60 g) buttermilk, plus more to thin if needed

1 clove garlic (about 3 g), mashed into a paste

2 tablespoons (6 g) finely chopped fresh chives

2 tablespoons (6 g) finely chopped fresh parsley

1 tablespoon (2 g) finely chopped fresh dill

2 tablespoons (30 g) fresh lemon juice (about 1 medium lemon)

½ teaspoon (2.5 g) Dijon mustard

½ teaspoon (1.5 g) Diamond Crystal kosher salt (see the salt conversion table on page 21 if using other salt)

¼ teaspoon (0.5 g) freshly ground black pepper

¼ teaspoon (1 g) onion powder

In a medium bowl, whisk together the mayonnaise, sour cream, and buttermilk until smooth. Add the mashed garlic and stir to combine. Mix in the chives, parsley, dill, lemon juice, Dijon, salt, pepper, and onion powder. Taste and adjust the seasoning as needed. For a thinner consistency, stir in a splash more buttermilk.

Cover and refrigerate for at least 30 minutes before serving to let the flavors meld.

Store in an airtight container in the refrigerator for up to 5 days. Stir before using.

NOTE: IF YOU DON'T HAVE BUTTERMILK ON HAND, MAKE YOUR OWN BY COMBINING ¼ CUP (60 G) WHOLE MILK WITH ¾ TEASPOON LEMON JUICE OR VINEGAR. LET IT SIT FOR 5 TO 10 MINUTES BEFORE USING.

VEGAN RANCH

The soaked cashews create a rich, velvety base for the same punchy, herby flavor profile as the dairy ranch recipe, so it's a good one to opt for when you're serving a crowd with mixed dietary needs. Your vegan/dairy-free friends will be thrilled to have something so delicious, and your dairy-loving friends will be none the wiser.

YIELD: ABOUT 1¼ CUPS

1 cup (135 g) raw cashews, soaked in water to cover for at least 4 hours or boiled for 10 minutes

½ cup (120 g) water, plus more to thin if needed

2 tablespoons (30 g) lemon juice

1 clove garlic (about 3 g), mashed into a paste

1 tablespoon (15 g) apple cider vinegar

1 teaspoon (5 g) Dijon mustard

2 tablespoons (6 g) finely chopped fresh chives

2 tablespoons (6 g) finely chopped fresh parsley

1 tablespoon (2 g) finely chopped fresh dill

½ teaspoon (1.5 g) Diamond Crystal kosher salt (see the salt conversion table on page 21 if using other salt)

¼ teaspoon (0.5 g) freshly ground black pepper

¼ teaspoon (1 g) onion powder

Drain and rinse the soaked cashews. In a blender, combine them with the water, lemon juice, garlic, apple cider vinegar, and Dijon mustard. Blend until completely smooth and creamy.

Stir in the chopped herbs, salt, pepper, and onion powder. Taste and adjust the seasoning. Thin with more water if desired.

Cover and refrigerate for at least 30 minutes before serving. Use as a dip, dressing, or spread. Keeps in the fridge for up to 5 days.

HOT HONEY

Sweet, spicy, and flavorful, this is the ultimate drizzle for anything that needs a fiery finish (literally everything, if you ask me). For most pizzas, Calabrian hot honey works well. Anything particularly umami-driven, like King's Pie (page 117), which we created with *Top Chef* Champion Melissa King, benefits from pleasantly numbing Szechuan peppercorns, along with some cloves, star anise, cinnamon, and a little vinegar. If you want the flavor of chiles but can't handle the heat, go for Aleppo pepper. Whatever direction you take, hot honey is an easy way to take your pizza to the next level, so get creative and play with your favorite flavorings.

YIELD: ABOUT 1 CUP

1 cup (340 g) mild honey

1 tablespoon heat source of choice, such as Calabrian chile paste, ground Szechuan peppercorns, dried, crushed jalapeños, or Aleppo pepper

1 tablespoon (2 g) crushed red chile flakes

Additional flavorings as desired (see below for guidance)

Gently warm the honey in a small saucepan over low heat. Stir in the heat source of choice, crushed red chile flakes, and any additional flavorings. Infuse over low heat for 5 to 7 minutes, stirring occasionally. Remove from the heat and let steep for 1 hour or more.

Strain for a smooth version or leave bits in for texture. Store in a sealed jar at room temperature for up to 2 months (or 1 month if solids remain).

For **Calabrian Chile-Garlic Hot Honey:** 1 tablespoon (about 15 g) Calabrian chile paste plus 1 clove garlic, lightly smashed

For **Szechuan Hot Honey:** 1 tablespoon (about 5 g) Szechuan peppercorns, 2 whole cloves, 1 star anise, 1 cinnamon stick, and 1½ tablespoons (22.5 g) distilled white vinegar

CILANTRO-LIME CREMA

Creamy, herbaceous, and tangy, this crema delivers a cool contrast to spicy toppings or rich meats. At the restaurant we use it as a dip and drizzle for pizza, as well as wings and fries. I also love it on tacos, nachos, and even grilled artichokes.

YIELD: ABOUT 2 CUPS

1½ cups (30 g) fresh cilantro, stems included, washed thoroughly

¼ cup (60 g) fresh lime juice (from about 2 limes)

½ cup (120 g) mayonnaise

1 teaspoon (3 g) Diamond Crystal kosher salt (see the salt conversion table on page 21 if using other salt)

½ cup (120 g) sour cream or full-fat Greek yogurt

In a blender or food processor, combine the cilantro, lime juice, mayonnaise, and salt. Blend until smooth and bright green, 1 to 2 minutes. Add the sour cream and blend briefly to combine.

Taste and adjust the salt or lime juice if needed.

Transfer to a clean jar and refrigerate. Keeps for up to 1 week.

SPG BBQ SAUCE

This sweet, tangy sauce is your go-to if you're looking for a classic American-style barbecue flavor with just a hint of smoke. The ketchup and brown sugar bring that familiar backyard vibe, while the sweet tomatoes keep the flavor squarely in pizza town. It's very minimally cooked, which helps keep it from becoming cloyingly sweet after cooking down further when the pizza it's on is baked. It's great on sausage pies, a classic barbecue chicken pizza, with grilled veggies, or even as a dip for crusts or Garlic Cheesy Bread (page 136).

YIELD: ABOUT 2½ CUPS

⅔ cup (160 g) ketchup

⅓ cup (80 g) apple cider vinegar

¼ cup (55 g) packed brown sugar

¼ cup (85 g) honey

¼ teaspoon (1 g) liquid smoke

½ teaspoon (1 g) smoked paprika

1 teaspoon (3 g) Diamond Crystal kosher salt (see the salt conversion table on page 21 if using other salt)

¼ teaspoon (0.5 g) freshly cracked black pepper

One 15-ounce (425 g) can crushed tomatoes

Combine all the ingredients in a small saucepan.

Bring to a boil over medium heat, then reduce to a simmer and cook for 5 minutes, stirring occasionally.

Remove from the heat and let cool to room temperature.

Taste and adjust the seasoning as needed.

Use immediately or store, covered, in the refrigerator for up to 5 days.

SZECHUAN CHILE OIL

This fragrant, spicy oil delivers a deep red color and signature numbing heat from Szechuan peppercorns. Use it as a drizzle for pizza, like the Szechuan Chicken Pie (page 114), dumplings, noodles, or roasted vegetables. This version includes two options: one with the chile sediment for bold flavor and texture and a strained version for a cleaner finish.

YIELD: ABOUT 1⅛ CUPS UNDRAINED OR 1 CUP DRAINED

1 cup (220 g) neutral oil, such as rice bran, canola, or grapeseed

3 cloves garlic (about 10 g), peeled and smashed

One 1-inch knob ginger (about 10 g), peeled and smashed

1 scallion (about 15 g), cut into 2 or 3 pieces

2 bay leaves (about 1 g)

1 star anise pod (about 1 g)

1 small cinnamon stick (about 3 g)

¼ teaspoon (about 0.5 g) whole cloves

¼ teaspoon (about 0.5 g) whole coriander seeds

¼ teaspoon (about 0.5 g) Szechuan peppercorns

Pinch (about 0.2 g) whole white peppercorns

Small handful (about 10 g) cilantro stems

6 tablespoons (30 g) Szechuan chile powder

¼ teaspoon (0.7 g) Diamond Crystal kosher salt (see the salt conversion table on page 21 if using other salt)

In a small saucepan, heat the oil over medium-high heat until it reaches 350°F.

Carefully add the garlic, ginger, and scallion. Fry for 2 minutes, stirring occasionally.

Add the bay leaves, star anise, cinnamon stick, cloves, coriander, Szechuan peppercorns, white peppercorns, and cilantro stems. Continue to fry for 2 to 3 minutes, stirring frequently, until the aromatics are deep golden brown but not burnt.

Remove from the heat. Use a spider or slotted spoon to remove and discard the solids.

Let the oil cool for about 5 minutes—if it's too hot, the chile powder will burn.

Add the chile powder and salt to a heatproof bowl. Carefully pour the warm oil over the chile powder, stirring gently. The oil will sizzle and become a deep shade of red. Let sit for 5 minutes to infuse.

Version 1 (Chunky): Leave the chile sediment in for a punchier, more rustic oil.

Version 2 (Smooth): Strain the finished oil through a fine-mesh sieve or cheesecloth for a cleaner texture.

Store in a sealed jar in the refrigerator for up to a month.

QUICK-PICKLED VEGETABLES

This quick-pickle method brings brightness, acidity, and crunch to pizzas, sandwiches, salads, and snack time in general. It's also a great way to save whatever veggies are lingering in your produce drawer, threatening to go bad. And if you have a garden, it's a life-saver. When a recipe in this book calls for pickled vegetables, this is the technique to use.

YIELD: ABOUT 2 CUPS

2 cups your choice of vegetables: red onions, cucumbers, carrots, radishes, chiles, cauliflower, green beans, cabbage, garlic cloves, bell peppers, zucchini, or anything else you can think of

1 cup (240 g) distilled white vinegar or apple cider vinegar

½ cup (120 g) water

1 tablespoon (10 g) Diamond Crystal kosher salt (see the salt conversion table on page 21 if using other salt)

1 tablespoon (12 g) sugar

Optional flavor add-ins: sliced garlic, black peppercorns, crushed red chile flakes, fresh dill, bay leaf, mustard seeds, or coriander seeds

Pack the cleaned vegetables into a jar or jars.

In a medium pot over high heat, stir the vinegar, water, salt, and sugar together for 2 to 3 minutes, until completely dissolved.

Pour the hot brine over the vegetable and add any add-ins. Let cool at room temperature with the lid(s) off.

Once the pickles cool to room temperature, screw the lid(s) on tightly and store in the fridge.

The pickles may be used as soon as they are thoroughly chilled, but will taste best after they've been refrigerated in the brine for 1 to 2 days.

OLD-SCHOOL PIES

Introduction

Before we get into the less orthodox pizzas we're known for at Square Pie Guys, I want to take a beat to honor the classics. After all, this chapter is all about foundational flavor combinations: the pies that taught me the basics of balancing flavor on a thick, frico-edged slab of dough.

We'll start, of course, with the most classic of classics: plain cheese pie, or what we call at SPG the Regular Square (page 74). You can do a lot to a plain cheese, like adding a stripy red top of cooked tomato sauce, or doing it Margherita-style, with fresh mozzarella and basil, or even a Sicilian-adjacent approach, inspired by the iconic squares at L&B Spumoni Gardens in Brooklyn. They're all cousins, really—variations on the idea of "cheese pizza" that manage to feel wildly different from one another depending on how you sauce and finish them.

Then there's The Pepperoni (page 83), because obviously. This is the classic cupped-edge, grease-laced situation we all dream about, and I'd argue it's one of the few foods on Earth that actually lives up to the hype. There's also The Liz (page 88), which is a white pie, made with my garlicky ricotta-based white sauce that bubbles up into something creamy, cheesy, and ever so slightly feral in its indulgence. The Garlicky Clam Pie (page 80) is my nod to New Haven (but better on a thick, crispy Detroit-style crust, if you ask me), and the Vodka Pie (page 82)—well, that one is a personal favorite. That creamy, tomatoey, ever so slightly spicy sauce sinks into the corners in a way that should probably be illegal. But lucky for us, it's not.

These pizzas are my take on the standards—the pies that gave me a blueprint for everything else. They're the reason the more experimental flavors in the next chapter work at all. Once you know how a cheese pie can sing in four or five different ways, or how garlic and seafood can behave on a square pie, you understand the rules deeply enough to break them.

REGULAR SQUARE 2 WAYS (PLAIN AND UPSIDE DOWN)

This is the foundational pie that started it all. This recipe offers a modular blueprint for four iconic variations: plain, red top, Margherita-style, and a version inspired by Brooklyn's L&B Spumoni Gardens. Whether you want something classic and saucy or fresh and basil-flecked, this is the base to build on. Play with the cheese layering and sauce placement to see just how different each style can feel. No matter which version you go with, you'll end up with a deeply satisfying slab of pizza.

YIELD: ONE 10-BY-14-INCH DETROIT-STYLE PIZZA

PIZZA

⅔ cup (167 g) Red Sauce (page 46)

One 10-by-14-inch dough of your choice, in the pan, proofed, and ready to use

1¾ cups (212 g) shredded medium cheddar

2⅛ cups (240 g) shredded or diced whole-milk low-moisture mozzarella

FOR THE TOP (AFTER BAKING)

4 tablespoons (63 g) Red Sauce (page 46, optional)

2 tablespoons (16 g) freshly grated Parmesan or Grana Padano

TO BUILD THE PIZZA

Arrange a rack at the bottom of your oven.

Preheat the oven to 550°F (or as high as it goes).

Ladle or spoon the Red Sauce across the top of the pie in a thin, even layer, going all the way to the edge.

Along the edges of the pan containing the dough, carefully sprinkle the cheddar in a tight collar to form a 1-inch border.

Working from the outside in, sprinkle the mozzarella over the cheddar and sauce. Some cheddar and sauce will peek through.

Bake the pizza for 15 to 18 minutes, or until the bottom of the crust is deep golden brown and the edges are crispy.

For a browner top, broil for 1 to 2 minutes until bubbly and browned in spots.

Remove from the oven and carefully transfer to a cooling rack. Let cool for 2 to 3 minutes, then transfer to a cutting board and cut into squares.

TO FINISH THE TOP

For an upside-down pie, spoon the additional Red Sauce over the baked pie.

Sprinkle with the Parmesan and serve immediately.

THE MVP

This glamorous pie offers an easy answer to the question, *What kind of sauce do you want on your pizza?*

Easy—all three: marinara, vodka, and pesto, aka the MVP! This pie embraces the upside-down sauce style, striping sauces over the top of a baked sauceless pie, a process we streamline at the restaurant by putting the sauces in squeeze bottles, but spooning them on or pouring from a spouted measuring cup works just as well.

YIELD: ONE 10-BY-14-INCH DETROIT-STYLE PIZZA

PIZZA

One 10-by-14-inch dough of your choice, in the pan, proofed, and ready to use

1¾ cups (212 g) shredded medium cheddar

2⅛ cups (240 g) cubed whole-milk low-moisture mozzarella

FOR THE TOP (AFTER BAKING)

⅓ cup (75 g) Red Sauce (page 46)

⅓ cup (75 g) Vodka Sauce (page 49)

⅓ cup (85 g) Fresh Herb Pesto (page 61)

2 tablespoons (16 g) freshly grated Parmesan or Grana Padano

TO BUILD THE PIZZA

Arrange a rack at the bottom of your oven.

Preheat the oven to 550°F (or as hot as your oven allows).

Along the edges of the pan containing the dough, carefully sprinkle the cheddar in a tight collar to form a 1-inch border.

Working from the outside in, sprinkle the mozzarella over the top of the dough.

Bake the pizza for 15 to 18 minutes, or until the bottom of the crust is deep golden brown and the edges are crispy.

For a browner top, broil for 1 to 2 minutes, until bubbly and browned in spots.

Remove from the oven and carefully transfer to a cooling rack to rest for 2 to 3 minutes, then transfer to a cutting board and cut into squares.

TO FINISH THE TOP

Drizzle the Red Sauce, Vodka Sauce, and Fresh Herb Pesto in alternating diagonal lines across the pie.

Sprinkle with the Parmesan and serve immediately.

DETROIT-STYLE MARGHERITA PIZZA

This pie reimagines the classic Margherita with a Detroit-style twist, balancing tomatoes and fresh mozzarella with the caramelized edges of cubed low-moisture cheese. The basil and olive oil go on at the end to keep their flavors sharp and clean, and it's a great reminder that elegance and indulgence can totally coexist.

YIELD: ONE 10-BY-14-INCH DETROIT-STYLE PIZZA

PIZZA

⅔ cup (167 g) Red Sauce (page 46)

One 10-by-14-inch dough of your choice, in the pan, proofed, and ready to use

1¾ cups (212 g) shredded medium cheddar cheese

1½ cups (150 g) shredded or diced whole-milk low-moisture mozzarella

⅔ cup (85 g) fresh whole-milk mozzarella, torn into 1-inch chunks

FOR THE TOP (AFTER BAKING)

Extra-virgin olive oil for drizzling

Fresh basil leaves, gently torn

A few pinches of flaky salt

TO BUILD THE PIZZA

Arrange a rack at the bottom of your oven.

Preheat the oven to 550°F (or as high as it goes).

Ladle or spoon the Red Sauce across the top of the pie in a thin, even layer, going all the way to the edge.

Along the edges of the pan containing the dough, carefully sprinkle the cheddar in a tight collar to form a 1-inch border.

Sprinkle the low-moisture mozzarella chunks over the cheddar border. Some cheddar and sauce will peek through.

Layer the fresh mozzarella over the sauce.

Bake for 15 to 20 minutes, until the cheese is bubbly and lightly browned and the corners are golden and crispy.

Remove from the oven and carefully transfer to a cooling rack to rest for 2 to 3 minutes, then transfer to a cutting board and cut into squares.

TO FINISH THE TOP

Drizzle with the olive oil and top with the basil and salt, then serve hot.

DETROIT-STYLE SPUMONI SQUARE

This one is an homage to the thick, saucy squares at L&B Spumoni Gardens in Brooklyn—a personal favorite of mine. Here, I've adapted the spirit of those iconic pies to the Detroit-style format, which means extra crunch and cheese-driven crust structure. It's bold, saucy, and super nostalgic for those of us who grew up on East Coast pizza. The original is made with deli-sliced low-moisture whole-milk mozzarella, a cooked tomato sauce over the cheese top, and finished with grated Pecorino Romano, which I use here. You can definitely use Grana Padano or Parmesan to finish, but I find that Pecorino brings a welcome sharpness that ties the whole thing together.

YIELD: ONE 10-BY-14-INCH DETROIT-STYLE PIZZA

1½ cups (337 g) Red Sauce (page 46)

One 10-by-14-inch dough of your choice in the pan, proofed, and ready to use

1¾ cups (212 g) shredded medium cheddar cheese

10 to 12 deli slices (240 g) low-moisture whole-milk mozzarella

¼ cup (27 g) grated Pecorino Romano, Grana Padano, or Parmesan

¼ teaspoon dried oregano

Arrange a rack at the bottom of your oven.

Preheat the oven to 550°F (or as hot as your oven allows).

Pour the sauce into a small pot and cook for 12 to 15 minutes over medium heat until thickened. Remove from the heat and set aside until ready to use.

Along the edges of the pan containing the dough, carefully sprinkle the cheddar in a tight collar to form a 1-inch border.

Working from the outside in, lay the mozzarella slices over the cheddar.

Bake the pizza for 15 to 18 minutes, or until the bottom of the crust is deep golden brown and the edges are browned and crispy.

Ladle the sauce generously over the cheese—yes, on top. Cover in bold vertical stripes or a full, even layer, L&B-style. Sprinkle with the Pecorino Romano and the dried oregano.

Return to the oven for another 7 to 10 minutes, until the sauce bubbles, the cheese melts into the corners, and the crust crisps up. Remove from the oven and carefully transfer to a cooling rack. Let rest for 2 to 3 minutes, then transfer to a cutting board and cut into squares.

GARLICKY CLAM PIE

An East Coast classic meets the crispy-bottomed heft of Detroit-style. The brininess of chopped clams pairs beautifully with garlic, lemon zest, and bubbling White Sauce, making this one of the most unexpectedly addictive pies we make. If you like a little ocean in your cheese, this one's a no-brainer. Eat this pie with cold white wine or a crisp pilsner.

YIELD: ONE 10-BY-14-INCH DETROIT-STYLE PIZZA

PIZZA

½ cup (128 g) White Sauce (page 50)

One 10-by-14-inch dough of your choice, in the pan, proofed, and ready to use

1¾ cups (212 g) shredded medium cheddar

2⅛ cups (240 g) shredded or diced whole-milk low-moisture mozzarella

One and a half 6.5-ounce cans clams (about 4¼ ounces or 120 grams clam meat total), drained and chopped

¼ teaspoon (0.7 g) Diamond Crystal kosher salt (see salt conversion table on page 21 if using other salt)

2 tablespoons (32 g) extra-virgin olive oil

3 cloves fresh garlic, chopped (about 6 g)

Zest of 1 large lemon (about 5 g)

FOR THE TOP (AFTER BAKING)

2 tablespoons (16 g) freshly grated Grana Padano or Parmesan

2 tablespoons (about 8 g) finely chopped fresh parsley leaves

OPTIONAL BUT RECOMMEND

A big pinch of crushed red chile flakes

A few extra pinches of lemon zest

TO BUILD THE PIZZA

Arrange a rack at the bottom of your oven and preheat to 550°F (or as hot as it goes).

Spread the White Sauce across the pie in a thin, even layer, going all the way to the edge.

Along the edges of the pan containing the dough, carefully sprinkle the cheddar in a tight collar to form a 1-inch border.

Sprinkle the mozzarella evenly over the sauce and cheddar.

In a small bowl, combine the chopped clams, kosher salt, olive oil, garlic, and lemon zest. Mix well and distribute evenly over the mozzarella.

Place in the oven and bake for 15 to 18 minutes, until the crust is golden and the cheese is bubbling.

Let rest on a cooling rack for 2 to 3 minutes, then cut into squares.

TO FINISH THE TOP

Sprinkle the Grana Padano and chopped parsley, and, if using, the crushed red chile flakes and lemon zest, evenly over the top and serve immediately.

VODKA PIE

If you ask me in front of an audience, I'll insist I love all my sauce children equally, but if you get me a little bit drunk and ask me in private, I'll whisper the truth, which is that I do, in fact, have a favorite child, and it's the spicy, creamy, tomato-sweet Vodka Sauce this pie is named for. This is a simple pizza—just Vodka Sauce and cheese, but when you want something comforting and flavorful, there's nothing better.

YIELD: ONE 10-BY-14-INCH DETROIT-STYLE PIZZA

PIZZA

¾ cup (180 g) Vodka Sauce (page 49)

One 10-by-14-inch dough of your choice, in the pan, proofed, and ready to use

1¾ cups (212 g) shredded medium cheddar

2⅛ cups (240 g) shredded or cubed whole-milk low-moisture mozzarella

FOR THE TOP (AFTER BAKING)

2 tablespoons (16 g) freshly grated Grana Padano or Parmesan

TO BUILD THE PIZZA

Arrange a rack at the bottom of your oven.

Preheat the oven to 550°F (or as hot as it goes).

Spoon the Vodka Sauce across the pie in a thin, even layer, going all the way to the edge. Along the edges of the pan containing the dough, carefully sprinkle the cheddar in a tight collar to form a 1-inch border.

Working from the outside in, scatter the low-moisture mozzarella evenly across the pie, from edge to edge (including over the cheddar border).

Bake the pizza for 15 to 18 minutes, or until the bottom of the crust is a deep golden brown and the edges are crispy.

For a browner top, broil for 1 to 2 minutes, until the cheese bubbles and browns in spots.

Remove from the oven and transfer to a cooling rack. Let cool for 2 to 3 minutes, then transfer to a cutting board and cut into squares.

TO FINISH THE TOP

Sprinkle with the Grana Padano and serve immediately.

THE PEPPERONI

This is the one. When people imagine Detroit-style pizza, they're usually picturing something like this: crispy frico edges, gooey center, and a full carpet of cupped, charred pepperoni. Personally, I think the pie's simplicity is perfect as it is, but if you want to go old-school and put the Red Sauce on top, I won't stop you.

YIELD: ONE 10-BY-14-INCH DETROIT-STYLE PIZZA

PIZZA

⅔ cup (167 g) Red Sauce (page 46)

One 10-by-14-inch dough of your choice, in the pan, proofed, and ready to use

1¾ cups (212 g) shredded medium cheddar

2⅛ cups (240 g) shredded or cubed whole-milk low-moisture mozzarella

72 slices (about 125 g) cup-and-char pepperoni

FOR THE TOP (AFTER BAKING)

2 tablespoons (16 g) freshly grated Parmesan or Grana Padano

TO BUILD THE PIZZA

Arrange a rack at the bottom of your oven and preheat to 550°F (or as hot as it goes).

Spoon the Red Sauce across the pie in a thin, even layer, going all the way to the edge.

Sprinkle the cheddar cheese around the edges of the pan containing the dough to form a tight 1-inch border. Working from the outside in, scatter the mozzarella evenly across the pie, from edge to edge, including over the cheddar border.

Layer the pepperoni tightly across the top of the pizza, edge to edge, covering the cheese and sauce completely.

Place the pan in the oven and bake for 15 to 18 minutes, until the crust is deep golden brown on the bottom and the edges are crispy.

For extra browning and bubbly cheese, broil for 1 to 2 minutes at the end.

Transfer the pizza to a cooling rack and let rest for 2 to 3 minutes, then transfer to a cutting board and cut into squares.

TO FINISH THE TOP

Sprinkle with the Parmesan and serve immediately.

THE ELLEN SUPREME

This is our everything-but-the-kitchen-sink pie—bold, salty, and packed with toppings that somehow all get along. Named after my friend Ellen, who taught me how to make vodka sauce, it combines sausage, pepperoni, pickled peppers, and caramelized onions over a Vodka-Sauced, cheese-laced crust. It's the kind of pizza that feels like a three-course meal in itself—and maybe a little like a 10-by-14-inch party, too. Best served hot and with lots of napkins.

YIELD: ONE 10-BY-14-INCH DETROIT-STYLE PIZZA

ONIONS

1 tablespoon (14 g) extra-virgin olive oil

1 medium yellow onion (about 125 g), chopped

¼ teaspoon (0.7 g) Diamond Crystal kosher salt (see the salt conversion table on page 21 if using other salt)

PIZZA

¾ cup (185 g) Vodka Sauce (page 49)

One 10-by-14-inch dough of your choice, in the pan, proofed, and ready to use

1¾ cups (212 g) shredded medium cheddar

2⅛ cups (240 g) shredded or diced whole-milk low-moisture mozzarella

¾ cup (about 100 g) uncooked Italian sausage (mild or spicy), cut into 1-inch pieces

42 slices (75 g) cup-and-char pepperoni

¼ cup (about 50 g) drained and chopped pickled red peppers (see page 71, or use store-bought, like Mama Lil's)

FOR THE TOP (AFTER BAKING)

2 tablespoons (16 g) freshly grated Grana Padano or Parmesan

2 tablespoons (16 g) chopped fresh parsley

TO PREPARE THE ONIONS

Heat a heavy-bottomed skillet over medium heat. Add the olive oil and onions. Cook for 5 to 7 minutes, stirring occasionally, until golden brown. Sprinkle with the salt and stir gently to combine.

Transfer the onions to a bowl and set aside.

TO BUILD THE PIZZA

Arrange a rack at the bottom of your oven and preheat it to 550°F (or as hot as your oven allows).

Spoon the Vodka Sauce across the top of the pie in a smooth, even layer.

Sprinkle the cheddar along the pan edges in a tight 1-inch border around the dough.

Sprinkle the mozzarella over the sauce and cheddar.

Add the cooked onions, sausage, pepperoni, and pickled peppers evenly.

Bake for 15 to 18 minutes, until golden and crispy at the edges. If you want a little more browning, broil for 2 to 3 minutes.

Remove the pizza from the oven and let rest for 2 to 3 minutes on a cooling rack, then transfer to a cutting board and cut into squares.

TO FINISH THE TOP

Sprinkle with the Grana Padano and parsley and serve.

THE GREEN PIE

This pie is proof that not every Detroit-style pizza has to be heavy. The sautéed kale and spoonfuls of herb pesto make it feel almost virtuous, while the creamy White Sauce and salty preserved lemon (or lemon zest, if that's what you've got) keep things punchy. It's rich but not overwhelming, green in every direction, and just the thing when you want your pizza to eat like a vegetable plate, only way better.

YIELD: ONE 10-BY-14-INCH DETROIT-STYLE PIZZA

KALE

1 tablespoon (14 g) extra-virgin olive oil

1 large bunch (about 100 g) dinosaur kale, ribs removed and leaves thinly sliced

¼ teaspoon (0.7 g) Diamond Crystal kosher salt (see the salt conversion table on page 21 if using other salt)

½ teaspoon (2 g) freshly ground black pepper

PIZZA

¾ cup (180 g) White Sauce (page 50)

One 10-by-14-inch dough of your choice, in the pan, proofed, and ready to use

1¾ cups (212 g) shredded medium cheddar

2⅛ cups (240 g) shredded or diced whole-milk low-moisture mozzarella

2 teaspoons (11 g) finely chopped preserved lemon (or the zest of half a lemon—about 1½ teaspoons or 3 g)

FOR THE TOP (AFTER BAKING)

¼ cup (60 g) Fresh Herb Pesto (page 61)

TO PREPARE THE KALE

In a medium skillet over medium heat, warm the olive oil. Add the kale and sauté until wilted and tender, 5 to 7 minutes. Season with salt and pepper to taste and let cool until you're ready to build the pizza.

TO BUILD THE PIZZA

Arrange a rack at the bottom of your oven and preheat it to 550°F (or as high as it goes).

Spoon the White Sauce across the pie in a smooth, even layer, going all the way to the edge.

Sprinkle the cheddar along the edges of the pan containing the dough in a tight 1-inch border.

Sprinkle the mozzarella over the sauce and cheddar.

Scatter the sautéed kale on top, then sprinkle with the preserved lemon.

Bake for 15 to 18 minutes, until golden and crispy at the edges.

Remove from the oven and transfer to a cooling rack for 2 to 3 minutes, then transfer to a cutting board and cut into squares.

TO FINISH THE TOP

Spoon dollops of the pesto over the top of each square and serve immediately.

THE LIZ

This pie was born from a customer request—and stuck around because it's so damn good and a total classic. Liz, one of our early regulars, asked for something that reminded her of the Old Forge double-crust white pies she grew up eating in Pennsylvania, and what we came up with is now a menu staple. It's all garlic, cheese, and crispy crust, finished with a sharp parsley-Grana sprinkle that cuts through the richness.

YIELD: ONE 10-BY-14-INCH DETROIT-STYLE PIZZA

PIZZA

2 tablespoons (32 g) extra-virgin olive oil

3 cloves garlic (about 9 g), finely chopped

1 cup (256 g) White Sauce (page 50)

One 10-by-14-inch dough of your choice, in the pan, proofed, and ready to use

1¾ cups (212 g) shredded medium cheddar

2½ cups (240 g) shredded or diced whole-milk low-moisture mozzarella

2 tablespoons (32 g) diced fresh mozzarella (½-inch cubes)

FOR THE TOP (AFTER BAKING)

2 tablespoons (16 g) freshly grated Grana Padano or Parmesan

2 tablespoons (about 8 g) finely chopped fresh parsley leaves

TO BUILD THE PIZZA

Position a rack at the bottom of your oven and preheat to 550°F (or as hot as your oven allows).

Combine the olive oil and garlic in a small bowl. Set aside until ready to use.

Spoon the White Sauce in a thin layer across the pie, going all the way to the edge.

Sprinkle the cheddar cheese around the edge of the pan containing the dough to create a tight 1-inch border.

Sprinkle the low-moisture mozzarella evenly over the sauce and cheddar. Dot with the diced fresh mozzarella.

Drizzle the garlic-oil mixture over the top of the pie.

Bake for 15 to 18 minutes, until the crust is golden and the cheese is bubbling and browned in spots. (Do not broil—the direct heat will make the garlic taste bitter.)

Transfer to a cooling rack and let rest for 2 to 3 minutes, then transfer to a cutting board and cut into squares.

TO FINISH THE TOP

Sprinkle the Grana Padano and chopped parsley evenly over the top and serve immediately.

SQUARE PIE GUYS
MEET THE GUYS

NEW CLASSICS

Introduction

If the old-school pies in the previous chapter were my spin on tradition-defining Detroit-style pies, then this chapter is about the pizza I started making once I learned that anything can be good on a pie if the flavors and textures can harmonize on key. The pies in this chapter feature lots of traditional pizza toppings (Italian sausage, pepperoni, Calabrian chiles, tomatoes, and more), but you'll also find a lot of unexpected ingredients (beets, jerk chicken, Szechuan chile–infused honey, and carnitas, to name a few).

The way I see it, even though they may be a bit offbeat, these pies still have a lot in common with old-school Detroit pizza, because the Detroit pie was the result of a traditional dish being prepared with stuff that represented the place and moment in time in which the cooks were living. At Buddy's on Six Mile, that meant baking a Sicilian pie in a blue steel drip tray from an auto factory, instead of the traditional cast-iron rectangular pan used in Italy, and it meant topping it with tangy Wisconsin brick cheese, instead of mozzarella di bufala. At Square Pie Guys, we like to reflect our surroundings in our pies, too, which means using flour milled in nearby Sonoma County, lots of fresh, locally grown produce that changes with the season, and flavor profiles that are reflective of the veritable melting pot of cultures in the Bay Area. Think of the recipes in this chapter as a culinary tour of San Francisco and its neighboring communities by way of Detroit, with a healthy dose of my New York roots thrown in, too.

One thing you may notice in this chapter is that many of the pizzas are topped with two different sauces—one that goes on before the pizza is cooked (usually a white, red, or vodka sauce) and a second that goes on after (like hot honey, ranch, or a vinaigrette), sometimes alongside other garnishes, like grated Grana Padano, fresh herbs, or pickled vegetables. While this is indeed different from most conventional Detroit-style pizza, like the Regular Square on page 74, which features tomato sauce on top of the cheese, it's still very much in keeping with the spirit of Detroit-style pizza. It's still crispy, cheesy, and saucy. It's still crazy good.

I'm a big believer in the idea that you've gotta learn the rules to break them; develop total reverence for tradition so you can turn around and be wildly irreverent.

Some of the pizzas in this chapter may be a little unexpected, but I'm confident they'll knock your socks off.

No matter where you stand on tradition, you can't argue with delicious.

BEET-AN-ESCA

If you your go-to pasta order is puttanesca, you need to try this pie. The creamy beet sauce adds color and subtle sweetness, creating a surprising yet balanced base that will convert even the most fervent beet skeptic. Castelvetrano olives, pickled peppers, and fresh cherry tomatoes enhance complexity with briny, tangy notes. A drizzle of SPG Salsa Verde completes the flavor symphony.

YIELD: ONE 10-BY-14-INCH DETROIT-STYLE PIZZA

PIZZA

¾ cup (180 g) Beet Cream (page 53)

One 10-by-14-inch dough of your choice, in the pan, proofed, and ready to use

1¾ cups (212 g) shredded medium cheddar

2½ cups (240 g) shredded or diced whole-milk low-moisture mozzarella cheese

2 tablespoons (30 g) chopped pickled peppers (see page 71, or use store-bought, like Mama Lil's)

3½ tablespoons (106 g) chopped Castelvetrano olives

¾ cup (112 g) halved cherry or grape tomatoes

FOR THE TOP (AFTER BAKING)

4 tablespoons (61 g) SPG Salsa Verde (page 55)

TO BUILD THE PIZZA

Arrange a rack at the bottom of your oven.

Preheat the oven to 550°F (or as high as it goes).

Ladle or spoon the Beet Cream across the pie in a thin, even layer, going all the way to the edges.

Along the edges of the pan containing the dough, carefully sprinkle the cheddar in a tight collar to form a 1-inch border.

Working from the outside in, sprinkle the low-moisture mozzarella over the cheddar and sauce. The cheddar and sauce will peep through a bit; the mozzarella should be distributed across the entire pie.

Sprinkle the chopped pickled peppers, Castelvetrano olives, and cherry tomatoes evenly over the cheese.

Bake the pizza for 15 to 18 minutes, or until the bottom of the crust is a deep golden brown and the edges of the pie are crispy.

If you want the top of the pizza to be a bit browner, turn on the broiler and cook the pizza beneath it for a minute or so, just until the cheese starts to bubble and brown in spots.

When the pizza is cooked, remove it from the oven and carefully transfer the pie to a cooling rack. Let cool for 2 to 3 minutes, then transfer to a cutting board and cut into squares.

TO FINISH THE TOP

Drizzle the pie with the SPG Salsa Verde and serve immediately.

MEAN GREEN SAUSAGE MACHINE

This pizza celebrates broccoli rabe, whose bitterness pairs perfectly with rich sausage and creamy White Sauce. Sure, calling this healthy would be wishful thinking, but those greens do make it feel kinda virtuous. Hot Honey finishes things off, bringing sweetness and heat. Opt for sweet Italian sausage, or go spicy if you dare.

YIELD: ONE 10-BY-14-INCH DETROIT-STYLE PIZZA

BROCCOLI RABE

4 tablespoons (56 g) extra-virgin olive oil

4 cloves garlic (about 12 g), thinly sliced

½ teaspoon (0.5 g) crushed red chile flakes

8 ounces (239 g) broccoli rabe, chopped

PIZZA

¾ cup (180 g) White Sauce (page 50)

One 10-by-14-inch dough of your choice, in the pan, proofed, and ready to use

1¾ cups (212 g) shredded medium cheddar

8 ounces (240 g) uncooked mild Italian sausage, casing removed, cut into 1-inch pieces

2⅛ cups (240 g) shredded or diced whole-milk low-moisture cheese

FOR THE TOP (AFTER BAKING)

4 tablespoons (61 g) Hot Honey (page 67)

TO PREPARE THE BROCCOLI RABE

Bring a large pot of salted water to a boil. Meanwhile, heat the olive oil and garlic in a large frying pan over medium heat until fragrant, 1 to 2 minutes. Stir in the red chile flakes and toast for 30 seconds, then remove the pan from the heat.

Boil the broccoli rabe until the stalks are tender, 1 to 2 minutes, then drain well. Transfer the rabe to the frying pan and toss over medium-low heat.

Cook, stirring occasionally, until the rabe is very tender, about 10 minutes. Let cool completely before building your pizza.

TO BUILD THE PIZZA

Arrange a rack at the bottom of the oven and preheat to 550°F (or its highest setting).

Spread the White Sauce in a thin, even layer on the dough. Along the pan edges, sprinkle the cheddar in a tight collar to form a 1-inch border. Distribute the uncooked sausage evenly across the pie.

Working from the outside in, sprinkle the mozzarella over the cheddar, sauce, and sausage. The other ingredients will peep through slightly. Scatter the broccoli rabe evenly across the cheese. Bake for 15 to 18 minutes, or until the bottom is deep golden brown and the edges are crispy.

If you want the top browner, broil for about a minute, until the cheese bubbles and browns in spots. When cooked, carefully transfer the pizza to a cooling rack.

Let cool for 2 to 3 minutes, then transfer to a cutting board and cut into squares.

TO FINISH THE TOP

Drizzle with Hot Honey and serve immediately.

SPICY PEPPERONI

Really good pepperoni is just a liiiiittle bit spicy, and this pie takes that to the next level with the addition of pickled jalapeños for heat and bite, plus a drizzle of Calabrian chile paste–spiked ranch. The jalapeños get pickled just enough to mellow their heat and add a little tang, and the result is spicy, savory, and hard to stop eating. If you like pizza that punches back, this is it.

YIELD: ONE 10-BY-14-INCH DETROIT-STYLE PIZZA

PIZZA

¾ cup (185 g) Vodka Sauce (page 49)

One 10-by-14-inch dough of your choice, in the pan, proofed, and ready to use

1¾ cups (212 g) shredded medium cheddar

2⅛ cups (240 g) shredded or diced whole-milk low-moisture mozzarella

⅓ cup (about 50 g) sliced pickled jalapeños, drained (use jarred/canned or make your own using the recipe for Quick-Pickled Vegetables on page 71)

72 slices (125 g) cup-and-char pepperoni

FOR THE TOP (AFTER BAKING)

3 tablespoons (48 g) House Ranch (page 64)

1 to 2 teaspoons (4 to 8 g) Calabrian chile paste

1 fresh jalapeño, thinly sliced (optional)

TO BUILD THE PIZZA

Position a rack at the bottom of the oven and preheat to 550°F (or as hot as it goes).

Spoon the Vodka Sauce across the pie in an even layer, going all the way to the edges.

Sprinkle the cheddar along the pan edges to form a tight 1-inch border around the dough.

Scatter the low-moisture mozzarella evenly across the pie, from edge to edge (including over the cheddar border).

Scatter the pickled jalapeños across the cheese layer, and layer the pepperonis tightly across the top.

Bake for 15 to 18 minutes, until the crust is golden brown and the edges are crispy.

For extra browning, broil for 1 to 2 minutes.

Let the pizza rest on a cooling rack for 2 to 3 minutes, then cut into squares.

TO FINISH THE TOP

While the pizza cools, whisk the House Ranch and Calabrian chile paste together and drizzle it over the top of the cooked, cut pizza.

Garnish with the fresh jalapeño, if desired.

Serve immediately.

J. LIN PIE

I'll never forget the day when, in the early days of our first location, basketball legend Jeremy Lin walked into Square Pie Guys and ordered a create-your-own pie. It was a unique pie—a White Sauce base, pepperoni, Green Goddess Caesar, and extra red chile flakes. I was too nervous to say hello that first day, but when he came back several more times and ordered the same thing, I finally pulled myself together and gathered up the nerve to introduce myself. He couldn't have been nicer, and we ended up teaming up on a pizza collab benefiting Jeremy's nonprofit, the Jeremy Lin Foundation, which raises money for underprivileged youth. It was a fun and delicious way to do some good and introduce the world to Jeremy's iconic toppings combo.

YIELD: ONE 10-BY-14-INCH DETROIT-STYLE PIZZA

PIZZA

¾ cup (180 g) White Sauce (page 50)

One 10-by-14-inch dough of your choice, in the pan, proofed, and ready to use

1¾ cups (212 g) shredded medium cheddar

2¼ cups (240 g) shredded or diced whole-milk low-moisture mozzarella

60 slices (105 g) cup-and-char pepperoni

FOR THE TOP (AFTER BAKING)

4 tablespoons (60 g) Green Goddess Caesar (page 62)

1 to 2 teaspoons (0.5 to 1 g) red chile flakes

2 tablespoons (16 g) freshly grated Grana Padano or Parmesan

TO BUILD THE PIZZA

Arrange a rack at the bottom of your oven.

Preheat the oven to 550°F (or as hot as it goes).

Ladle or spoon the White Sauce across the top of the pie and use the back of the ladle or spoon to gently spread it into a thin, even layer.

Along the edges of the pan containing the dough, carefully sprinkle the cheddar in a tight collar to form a 1-inch border.

Working from the outside in, sprinkle the low-moisture mozzarella over the cheddar and sauce. The other ingredients will peep through a bit; the mozzarella should be distributed across the pie.

Arrange the pepperoni across the mozzarella in 6 rows of 10.

Bake the pizza for 15 to 18 minutes, or until the bottom of the crust is a deep golden brown and the edges of the pie are crispy.

If you want the top of the pizza to be a bit browner, turn on the broiler and cook the pizza beneath it for a minute or so, just until the cheese starts to bubble and brown in spots.

When the pizza is cooked, remove it from the oven and transfer carefully to a cooling rack. Let cool for 2 to 3 minutes, then transfer to a cutting board and cut into squares.

TO FINISH THE TOP

Drizzle the pie with the Green Goddess Caesar, sprinkle with the red chile flakes and Grana Padano and serve immediately.

YARDBIRD

This pizza was born of a collaboration with Chefs Solomon Johnson and Mike Woods of The Bussdown in Oakland, a phenomenal Afro-Caribbean soul food spot that is sadly now closed. Their jerk chicken inspired this fusion pie, which combines bold Caribbean flavor with creamy Vodka Sauce and spicy-sweet green sauce. It might sound a little wild, but trust—the heat, the creaminess, and the cheddar crust balance one another brilliantly.

YIELD: ONE 10-BY-14-INCH DETROIT-STYLE PIZZA

JERK CHICKEN

1 tablespoon (3 g) jerk seasoning

½ teaspoon (2 g) sugar

8 ounces (240 g) boneless, skin-on chicken thighs

1 tablespoon (14 g) neutral oil

ONIONS

1 tablespoon (14 g) extra-virgin olive oil

1¾ cups (255 g) chopped yellow onion

¼ teaspoon (0.7 g) kosher salt (see the salt conversion table on page 21 if using other salt)

PIZZA

⅔ cup (160 g) Vodka Sauce (page 49)

One 10-by-14-inch dough of your choice, in the pan, proofed, and ready to use

1¾ cups (212 g) shredded medium cheddar

2⅛ cups (240 g) shredded or diced whole-milk low-moisture mozzarella

2 tablespoons (30 g) chopped pickled peppers (see page 71, or use store-bought, like Mama Lil's)

FOR THE TOP (AFTER BAKING)

3 tablespoons (42 g) Kijani Kibichi Green Sauce (page 56)

TO PREPARE THE JERK CHICKEN

Preheat the oven to 550°F (or as high as it goes).

Line a rimmed baking sheet with parchment or aluminum foil.

Place the jerk seasoning and sugar in a small bowl and stir to combine.

Put the chicken thighs in a medium mixing bowl and drizzle the oil on top. Use clean hands to mix well, ensuring that the thighs are evenly coated.

Sprinkle the jerk-sugar mixture over the chicken and use clean hands to rub it all over the thighs.

Arrange the thighs skin-side down on the prepared baking sheet and bake for 10 to 12 minutes, until browned and cooked through—an instant-read thermometer should read at least 160°F.

Let the chicken cool on a tray, a plate, or a cooling rack for 5 minutes. or until cool enough to handle.

Chop into 1-inch cubes and set aside until you're ready to build the pizza.

TO PREPARE THE ONIONS

Heat a large, heavy-bottomed frying pan over medium heat. Add the olive oil, then add the onion and cook for 5 to 7 minutes, stirring occasionally, just until the onions begin to turn golden brown. Sprinkle the salt over the onions and stir gently to combine.

Transfer the onions to a bowl or other container until ready to build the pizza.

CONTINUED

TO BUILD THE PIZZA

Arrange a rack at the bottom of your oven and preheat it to 550°F (or as hot as your oven allows).

Ladle or spoon the Vodka Sauce within the cheese border and use the back of the ladle or spoon to gently spread it into a thin, even layer.

Along the edges of the pan containing the dough, carefully sprinkle the cheddar in a tight collar to form a 1-inch border.

Scatter the cooked onions and cooked, chopped chicken across the cheddar and sauce.

Working from the outside in, sprinkle the low-moisture mozzarella over the entirety of the pie. The toppings will peep through a bit; the mozzarella should be distributed across the pie.

Sprinkle the chopped pickled peppers evenly over the cheese.

Bake the pizza for 15 to 18 minutes, or until the bottom of the crust is a deep golden brown and the edges of the pie are crispy.

If you want the top of the pizza to be a bit browner, turn on the broiler and cook the pizza beneath it for a minute or so, just until the cheese starts to bubble and brown in spots.

When the pizza is cooked, remove it from the oven and transfer carefully to a cooling rack. Let cool for 2 to 3 minutes, then transfer to a cutting board and cut into squares.

TO FINISH THE TOP

Drizzle the pie with the Kijani Kibichi Green Sauce and serve immediately.

NORTH STATION PLAZA PIE

This pie is an homage to Richard Schechter, respected dentist, friend to many, and father to me. His passion for a corner slice of pan-baked pizza is almost as fervent as his profound love of shaved white onions. This pie—which, like the one on page 79, riffs on the iconic Sicilian at L&B Spumoni Gardens—honors both the man and the allium. The thinly sliced white onions (use a mandoline if you've got one) go onto the pizza raw, but they soften and sweeten in the oven and contrast beautifully with the pie's cheddar frico crust.

YIELD: ONE 10-BY-14-INCH DETROIT-STYLE PIZZA

PIZZA

1½ cups (350 g) Red Sauce (page 46)

One 10-by-14-inch dough of your choice, in the pan, proofed, and ready to use

1¾ cups (212 g) shredded medium cheddar

10 to 12 deli slices (240 g) whole-milk low-moisture mozzarella

1 large white onion (about 200 g), very thinly sliced

1 tablespoon (2 g) chopped fresh oregano or 1 teaspoon (0.5 g) dried

1 tablespoon (14 g) extra-virgin olive oil

TO FINISH

2 tablespoons (12 g) grated Pecorino Romano

2 tablespoons (3 g) torn fresh basil leaves for garnish

TO BUILD THE PIZZA

Arrange a rack at the bottom of your oven.

Preheat the oven to 550°F (or as hot as your oven allows).

Pour the sauce into a small pot and cook for 12 to 15 minutes over medium-high heat until thickened. Remove from the heat and set aside until ready to use.

Along the edges of the pan containing the dough, carefully sprinkle the cheddar in a tight collar to form a 1-inch border.

Top the dough with the mozzarella, spreading it all the way to the edges.

Spoon the Red Sauce across the top and use the back of a spoon or a rubber spatula to gently spread it over the top of the cheese.

Scatter the onions evenly across the surface.

Sprinkle with the oregano, then drizzle the olive oil over the top.

Bake for 15 to 18 minutes, until the cheddar crust is crisp and golden, the mozzarella is bubbling, and the onions have just begun to brown on top.

Remove from the oven, transfer to a cooling rack, and let rest for 2 to 3 minutes. Then transfer to a cutting board and cut into squares.

TO FINISH THE TOP

Sprinkle the Pecorino Romano over the top, then garnish with the basil and serve.

SUMMER TOMATO PIE

Developed with culinary icon and our friend Samin Nosrat, this pie is a love letter to tomato season. Using cherry tomatoes two ways—marinated fresh and confited with garlic—highlights their sweetness and acidity. A creamy White Sauce and pickled peppers add depth. Use sweet, butter-yellow Sungolds if possible; they're outrageously good on this pie. Make it when tomatoes are at their absolute best.

YIELD: ONE 10-BY-14-INCH DETROIT-STYLE PIZZA

MARINATED TOMATO SALSA

1 teaspoon (4 g) Calabrian chile paste

1 handful (about 15 g) chopped fresh basil leaves

1 cup (159 g) halved cherry or grape tomatoes

2 cloves (about 6 g) garlic, minced

¼ teaspoon (0.7 g) Diamond Crystal kosher salt (see the salt conversion table on page 21 if using other salt)

¼ teaspoon (1 g) freshly ground black pepper

1 tablespoon (14 g) lemon juice

PIZZA

⅔ cup (180 g) White Sauce (page 50)

One 10-by-14-inch dough of your choice, in the pan, proofed, and ready to use

1¾ cups (212 g) shredded medium cheddar

2⅛ cups (240 g) shredded or cubed whole-milk low-moisture mozzarella

½ cup (125 g) Tomato Confit (page 59), strained from the oil

2 tablespoons (30 g) chopped pickled peppers (see page 71, or use store-bought, like Mama Lil's)

TO MAKE THE MARINATED TOMATO SALSA

Combine all the ingredients in a bowl and stir gently to combine. Let marinate for at least an hour (or as long as 12 hours).

TO BUILD THE PIZZA

Arrange a rack at the bottom of your oven.

Preheat the oven to 550°F (or as hot as your oven allows).

Ladle or spoon the White Sauce across the pie and use the back of the ladle or spoon to gently spread it into a thin, even layer all the way to the edge.

Along the edges of the pan containing the dough, carefully sprinkle the cheddar in a tight collar to form a 1-inch border.

Working from the outside in, sprinkle the low-moisture mozzarella over the cheddar and sauce. The cheddar and sauce will peep through a bit; the mozzarella should be distributed across the pie.

Scatter the Tomato Confit and chopped pickled peppers evenly over the cheese.

Bake the pizza for 15 to 18 minutes, or until the bottom of the crust is a deep golden brown and the edges of the pie are crispy.

If you want the top of the pizza to be a bit browner, turn on the broiler and cook the pizza beneath it for a minute or so, just until the cheese starts to bubble and brown in spots.

When the pizza is cooked, remove it from the oven and transfer carefully to a cooling rack. Let cool for 2 to 3 minutes, then transfer to a board and cut into squares.

Use a slotted spoon to arrange the Marinated Tomato Salsa on top of the cut squares of pie.

Serve immediately.

ELOTE PIE

Inspired by Mexican street corn, this pie is creamy, spicy, and rich, with just enough tang and sweetness to make it addictive. Cotija cream stands in for mayo, Tajín adds a chile-lime kick, and roasted corn delivers a smoky-sweet crunch. Parbake the crust so it doesn't sag under the toppings. Save this one for corn season—or use frozen kernels in winter.

YIELD: ONE 10-BY-14-INCH DETROIT-STYLE PIZZA

ROASTED CORN

1¾ cups (267 g) fresh or thawed corn kernels

1 tablespoon (14 g) extra-virgin olive oil

¼ teaspoon (0.7 g) Diamond Crystal kosher salt (see the salt conversion table on page 21 if using other salt)

COTIJA CREAM

¼ cup (30 g) crumbled cotija cheese

¼ cup (30 g) whole-milk ricotta

3 tablespoons (48 g) heavy cream

¼ teaspoon (0.7 g) Diamond Crystal kosher salt (see the salt conversion table on page 21 if using other salt)

1¼ teaspoons (4 g) Tajín or taco seasoning

1½ tablespoons (24 g) lemon juice

PIZZA

One 10-by-14-inch dough of your choice, in the pan, proofed, and ready to use

1¾ cups (212 g) shredded medium cheddar

2⅛ cups (240 g) shredded or cubed whole-milk low-moisture mozzarella

1 cup (128 g) halved cherry or grape tomatoes

TO PREPARE THE ROASTED CORN

Preheat the oven to 550°F (or as hot as your oven allows).

In a medium mixing bowl, toss the corn kernels with the olive oil and salt.

Spread the corn on a baking sheet and bake for 6 to 8 minutes, stirring occasionally, until the corn begins to brown. Let cool on the tray or on a plate until you're ready to build the pizza.

TO PREPARE THE COTIJA CREAM

Combine all the ingredients in a blender or food processor and pulse just until a thick cream forms. Transfer to a bowl and set aside until ready to build the pizza.

TO BUILD THE PIZZA

Arrange a rack at the bottom of your oven. Preheat the oven to 550°F (or as high as it goes).

Parbake the dough for 4 to 6 minutes, just until it begins to turn brown.

Remove the pan from the oven and let cool for a few minutes, until warm to the touch.

Ladle or spoon the cotija cream across the pie and use the back of the ladle or spoon to gently spread it into a thin, even layer.

Along the edges of the pan containing the dough, carefully sprinkle the cheddar in a tight collar to form a 1-inch border.

Working from the outside in, sprinkle the low-moisture mozzarella over the entirety of the pie. The cotija cream will peep through a bit; the mozzarella should be distributed across the pie.

Scatter the halved tomatoes evenly across the pie.

FOR THE TOP (AFTER BAKING)

3 tablespoons (50 g) Cilantro-Lime Crema (page 68)

¼ cup (30 g) crumbled cotija

1¼ teaspoons (4 g) Tajín or taco seasoning

Bake the pizza for 15 to 18 minutes, or until the bottom of the crust is a deep golden brown and the edges of the pie are crispy.

If you want the top of the pizza to be a bit browner, turn on the broiler and cook the pizza beneath it for a minute or so, just until the cheese starts to bubble and brown in spots.

When the pizza is cooked, remove it from the oven and transfer carefully to a cooling rack. Let cool for 2 to 3 minutes, then transfer to a cutting board and cut into squares.

TO FINISH THE TOP

Drizzle the pie with the Cilantro-Lime Crema and sprinkle the cotija across the top.

Dust with the tajín and serve immediately.

NICE JEWISH PIE

Takeout played a big part in my childhood—my parents both worked late, and, growing up, I ate more than a few Reuben sandwiches from our local Jewish deli for dinner. This pizza may be a little unorthodox (in more than a few ways), but if the idea of an open-faced Reuben on a Detroit-style crust appeals to you, you've got to try it. It's got caraway for that classic rye bread flavor, plenty of pastrami, the unmistakable tang of sauerkraut, and a blend of Swiss and just enough mozzarella to tame the funk.

YIELD: ONE 10-BY-14-INCH DETROIT-STYLE PIZZA

PIZZA

¾ cup (180 g) White Sauce (page 50)

One 10-by-14-inch dough of your choice, in the pan, proofed, and ready to use

1¾ cups (212 g) shredded medium cheddar

1¼ cups (115 g) shredded or cubed whole-milk low-moisture mozzarella

1¼ cups (115 g) shredded or cubed Swiss cheese

6 ounces (160 g) sliced pastrami, cut into thin ribbons

RUSSIAN DRESSING

2 tablespoons (30 g) mayonnaise

1 tablespoon (15 g) ketchup

1 teaspoon (5 g) prepared horseradish

¼ teaspoon (1 g) Worcestershire sauce

Pinch of smoked paprika

Pinch of kosher salt

Dash of hot sauce (optional)

FOR THE TOP (AFTER BAKING)

2 tablespoons (30 g) pickled red onions (see page 71, or use store-bought)

2 tablespoons (30 g) drained sauerkraut

½ teaspoon (1 g) caraway seeds

8 or 9 small sprigs fresh dill

TO BUILD THE PIZZA

Arrange a rack at the bottom of your oven.

Preheat the oven to 550°F (or as hot as your oven allows).

Ladle or spoon the White Sauce and use the back of the ladle or spoon to gently spread it into a thin, even layer.

Along the edges of the pan containing the dough, carefully sprinkle the cheddar in a tight collar to form a 1-inch border.

Working from the outside in, sprinkle the low-moisture mozzarella over the cheddar and sauce.

Repeat with the Swiss cheese. The cheddar and sauce will peep through the cubed mozzarella and Swiss, but both should be distributed across the pie.

Bake the pizza for 8 to 10 minutes, or until it begins to bubble, then remove from the oven and scatter the pastrami across the top.

Return to the oven and bake for another 7 to 10 minutes, until the bottom of the crust is a deep golden brown and the edges of the pie are crispy.

TO MAKE THE RUSSIAN DRESSING

While the pizza cooks, whisk the Russian dressing ingredients together in a small bowl and set aside.

When the pizza is cooked, remove it from the oven and transfer carefully to a cooling rack. Let cool for 2 to 3 minutes, then transfer to a cutting board and cut into squares.

TO FINISH THE TOP

Drizzle the pie with the Russian Dressing, then scatter the pickled onions, sauerkraut, caraway seed, and fresh dill evenly across the top of the pie and serve immediately.

ZAZA "PIE" CHULIA

Named after Georgian-born NBA champ Zaza Pachulia, who helped us create this pie, this pizza is bold, balanced chaos. Herbed chicken, charred pineapple, Red Sauce, pepperoni, jalapeños, and spicy ranch shouldn't work together, but they do. It's smoky, sweet, savory, spicy—and somehow still clean-tasting. When we launched this, it became an instant hit.

YIELD: ONE 10-BY-14-INCH DETROIT-STYLE PIZZA

HERB CHICKEN

2 boneless, skinless chicken thighs (about 8 ounces or 240 g)

1 tablespoon (14 g) extra-virgin olive oil, plus more for drizzling

¾ teaspoon (3 g) kosher salt (see the salt conversion table on page 21 if using other salt)

1 teaspoon (3 g) dried oregano

2 cloves garlic (about 6 g), minced

Zest and juice of ½ medium lemon (about 1½ tablespoons juice and 1½ teaspoons zest)

¼ teaspoon (1 g) black pepper

CHARRED PINEAPPLE

One 8-ounce can (240 g) pineapple chunks, drained

TO PREPARE THE CHICKEN

Preheat the oven to 450°F.

Place the chicken thighs on a rimmed baking tray and drizzle with the oil.

Use clean hands to distribute the olive oil all over the thighs.

Sprinkle the thighs with the salt and arrange on the baking tray.

Roast the thighs for 18 to 20 minutes, until an internal thermometer registers at least 160°F.

While the chicken roasts, whisk together the remaining 1 tablespoon (14 g) oil, oregano, garlic, lemon zest and juice, and black pepper in a bowl.

Once the chicken is finished cooking, let it rest for 10 minutes, then remove the skin and chop the meat into 1-inch pieces.

Toss the chicken with the marinade and let sit until ready to prepare the pizza. (If you won't be making the pizza within the hour, store the chicken in the refrigerator.)

TO PREPARE THE PINEAPPLE

Preheat the oven to 550°F (or as hot as your oven allows).

Drain the pineapple and cut each chunk in half, so the pieces are no larger than ½ inch.

Line a rimmed baking sheet with parchment or aluminum foil and spread the pineapple chunks evenly across it.

Bake for 6 to 8 minutes, or until the pineapple begins to brown.

Drain any additional juice that cooks out and set the pineapple aside until ready to build the pizza.

PIZZA

⅔ cup (181 g) Red Sauce (page 46)

One 10-by-14-inch dough of your choice, in the pan, proofed, and ready to use

1¾ cups (212 g) shredded medium cheddar

2¼ cups (240 g) shredded or diced whole-milk low-moisture mozzarella

35 slices (60 g) cup-and-char pepperoni

2 tablespoons (30 g) pickled jalapeños (see the Quick-Pickled Vegetables recipe on page 71, or use store-bought)

FOR THE TOP (AFTER BAKING)

3 tablespoons (48 g) House Ranch (page 64)

1 to 2 teaspoons (4 to 8 g) Calabrian chile paste

TO BUILD THE PIZZA

Arrange a rack at the bottom of your oven.

Preheat the oven to 550°F (or as high as it goes).

Ladle or spoon the Red Sauce across the whole pie, and use the back of the ladle or spoon to gently spread it into a thin, even layer.

Along the edges of the pan containing the dough, carefully sprinkle the cheddar in a tight collar to form a 1-inch border.

Distribute the chopped chicken across the cheddar and sauce in an even layer.

Working from the outside in, sprinkle the low-moisture mozzarella over the cheddar, sauce, and chicken. The toppings will peep through a bit; the mozzarella should be distributed across the pie.

Sprinkle the charred pineapple across the pie.

Carefully arrange the pepperoni in 5 rows of 7.

Scatter the pickled jalapeños evenly across the pie.

Bake the pizza for 12 to 18 minutes, or until the bottom of the crust is a deep golden brown and the edges of the pie are crispy.

If you want the top of the pizza to be a bit browner, turn on the broiler and cook the pizza beneath it for a minute or so, just until the cheese starts to bubble and brown in spots (but be careful not to burn the pepperoni).

When the pizza is cooked, remove it from the oven and transfer carefully to a cooling rack. Let cool for 2 to 3 minutes.

TO FINISH THE TOP

In a small bowl, whisk the House Ranch and Calabrian chile paste together and drizzle it over the top of the cooked pizza.

Cut into squares and serve immediately.

PORK AND PINEAPPLE

My passion for the Vodka Sauce that forms the base of this pie was first ignited when I was in middle school and attending a lot of bar and bat mitzvah parties. While my Hebrew school classmates hit the dance floor, I always made a beeline for the ubiquitous pasta bar for a big bowl of penne alla vodka. I couldn't get enough of that creamy, slightly spicy tomato goodness, and I've been obsessed ever since. Here, slow-cooked carnitas meets tangy pineapple, jalapeños, and, of course, Vodka Sauce for a mashup of Italian and Mexican. It's a perfect blend of sweet and heat, and, just like my former thirteen-year-old self, it's great for parties—awkward dance moves optional.

YIELD: ONE 10-BY-14-INCH DETROIT-STYLE PIZZA

CARNITAS

8 ounces (240 g) pork loin roast

1½ teaspoons (4½ g) kosher salt (see the salt conversion table on page 21 if using other salt), divided

½ teaspoon (about 1 g) freshly ground black pepper

1 tablespoon (14 g) extra-virgin olive oil

1 teaspoon (3 g) smoked paprika

1 teaspoon (3 g) dried oregano

1 teaspoon (3 g) ground cumin

¼ teaspoon (1 g) cayenne pepper

1 small jalapeño (about 16 g), minced

3 cloves garlic (about 9 g), minced

1 cup (160 g) finely chopped white or yellow onion

½ cup (120 g) pilsner beer

⅓ cup (120 g) orange juice

PINEAPPLE

One 8-ounce (240 g) can pineapple chunks, drained

TO MAKE THE CARNITAS

Preheat the oven to 325°F (or set a slow cooker on high heat).

Season the pork with ½ teaspoon each of salt and pepper.

Heat a large pan over medium-high heat and pour the olive oil in. When the oil is hot, sear the pork on all sides until nicely browned, about 2 minutes per side.

Remove the pan from the heat and set it aside.

Add the remaining 1 teaspoon (3 g) of salt, spices, jalapeño, garlic, white onion, beer, and orange juice to the pan (or the slow cooker). Cover the pan with a fitted lid or aluminum foil and cook for 2½ to 3 hours, or until the pork is easy to shred. (If using a slow cooker, cook on high for 1 hour, then turn to low for 3 hours.)

Shred the pork inside the pan or slow cooker.

Let it rest, uncovered, in the sauce until ready to use.

TO PREPARE THE PINEAPPLE

Preheat the oven to 550°F (or as hot as your oven allows).

Drain the pineapple and cut each chunk in half, so the pieces are no larger than ½ inch.

Line a rimmed baking sheet with parchment or aluminum foil and spread the pineapple chunks evenly across it.

Bake for 6 to 8 minutes, or until the pineapple begins to brown.

Drain any additional juice that cooks out and set the pineapple aside until ready to build the pizza.

CONTINUED

PIZZA

⅔ cup (185 g) Vodka Sauce (page 49)

One 10-by-14-inch dough of your choice, in the pan, proofed, and ready to use

1¾ cups (212 g) shredded medium cheddar

2¼ cups (240 g) shredded or diced whole-milk low-moisture mozzarella

2 tablespoons (30 g) pickled jalapeños (see page 71, or use store-bought)

FOR THE TOP (AFTER BAKING)

About 2 tablespoons (27 g) finely diced white onion

Small handful chopped fresh cilantro leaves

Jalapeño pickling liquid

TO BUILD THE PIZZA

Arrange a rack at the bottom of your oven.

Preheat the oven to 550°F (or as high as it goes).

Ladle or spoon the Vodka Sauce across the pie and use the back of the ladle or spoon to gently spread it into a thin, even layer.

Along the edges of the pan containing the dough, carefully sprinkle the cheddar in a tight collar to form a 1-inch border.

Working from the outside in, sprinkle the mozzarella over the cheddar and sauce. The cheddar and sauce will peep through a bit; the mozzarella should be distributed across the pie.

Distribute the shredded carnitas across the pie.

Sprinkle the charred pineapple across the pie.

Distribute the pickled jalapeños across the pie.

Bake the pizza for 15 to 18 minutes, or until the bottom of the crust is a deep golden brown and the edges of the pie are crispy.

If you want the top of the pizza to be a bit browner, turn on the broiler and cook the pizza beneath it for a minute or so, just until the cheese starts to bubble and brown in spots.

When the pizza is cooked, remove it from the oven and transfer carefully to a cooling rack. Let cool for 2 to 3 minutes.

TO FINISH THE TOP

Sprinkle the onions and cilantro across the pie, along with a few spoonfuls of jalapeño pickling liquid.

Cut into squares and serve immediately.

NOTE: SOMETIMES I MAKE MY OWN CARNITAS AS PER THE RECIPE, BUT JUST AS OFTEN, I'LL SWING BY MY FAVORITE TAQUERIA TO PICK SOME UP AND SAVE MYSELF SOME TIME AND EFFORT.

DON'T GO BACON MY HEART

This one's an ode to my childhood obsession with bacon. With smoky bacon lardons, earthy kale, and cherry tomatoes for brightness, this pizza has all the smoke and richness you expect from a classic bacon pie, but the acidity and freshness of the kale and tomatoes keep it light enough to keep you coming back for another bite without being overwhelmed. Don't skip the final broil for extra-crispy lardons.

YIELD: ONE 10-BY-14-INCH DETROIT-STYLE PIZZA

⅔ cup (167 g) Red Sauce (page 46)

One 10-by-14-inch dough of your choice, in the pan, proofed, and ready to use

2¼ cups (212 g) shredded medium cheddar

1 large bunch (about 100 g) dinosaur kale, ribs removed and leaves thinly sliced

2¼ cups (240 g) shredded or diced whole-milk low-moisture mozzarella

About 1 cup (200 g) bacon lardons

¾ cup (106 g) cherry or grape tomatoes, halved

Arrange a rack at the bottom of your oven.

Preheat the oven to 550°F (or as hot as it goes).

Ladle or spoon the Red Sauce across the whole pie, going all the way to the edge, using the back of the ladle or spoon to gently spread it into a thin, even layer.

Along the edges of the pan containing the dough, carefully sprinkle the cheddar in a tight collar to form a 1-inch border.

Scatter the kale across the cheddar and sauce, from edge to edge of the pie.

Working from the outside in, sprinkle the low-moisture mozzarella over the cheddar, sauce, and kale. The cheddar, sauce, and kale will peep through a bit; the mozzarella should be distributed across the pie.

Top the cheese with the lardons and tomatoes, again working from edge to edge, so the toppings are distributed across the pie.

Bake the pizza for 15 to 18 minutes, or until the bottom of the crust is a deep golden brown and the edges of the pie are crispy.

If you want the top of the pizza to be a bit browner, turn on the broiler and cook the pizza beneath it for a minute or so, just until the cheese starts to bubble and brown in spots and the lardons get crispy.

When the pizza is cooked, remove it from the oven and transfer carefully to a cooling rack. Let cool for 2 to 3 minutes, then transfer to a cutting board, cut into squares, and serve immediately.

SZECHUAN CHICKEN PIE

During the 2020 pandemic lockdown, we experimented with selling hot chicken sandwiches. This pie captures the flavor profile of one of our best-selling sandwiches. Panko-coated and fried chicken thighs sit on a White Sauce base with jalapeños, chile oil, and a tangy sesame oil mayo. It's a little unconventional, but it really works. I like to cut this one into 2-inch squares and serve it as an appetizer with cold beer at parties.

YIELD: ONE 10-BY-14-INCH DETROIT-STYLE PIZZA

CHICKEN THIGHS

Neutral oil for frying

¼ cup (32 g) all-purpose flour

1 large egg, lightly beaten

2¾ cups (138 g) panko breadcrumbs

2 boneless, skinless chicken thighs (about 8 ounces or 240 g)

½ teaspoon (1.5 g) Diamond Crystal kosher salt (see the salt conversion table on page 21 if using other salt), plus more for seasoning

¼ teaspoon (1 g) black pepper

TO PREPARE THE CHICKEN

Fill a large cast-iron or heavy skillet with ⅓ inch of oil. Heat over medium heat until an instant-read thermometer registers 350°F.

Arrange the flour, the beaten egg, and the breadcrumbs in three separate wide, shallow bowls or large plates.

Place one chicken thigh between two pieces of parchment paper and use a mallet or rolling pin to gently pound the thigh to ½ inch thick. Repeat with the second thigh.

Season the chicken with the salt and pepper.

Working with one thigh at a time, dredge in the flour until fully coated, then shake off the excess.

Dip in the egg, coating both sides, let the excess drip off, then press into the breadcrumbs until well coated.

Transfer to a clean plate and repeat with the remaining thigh.

Fry the chicken thighs until their bottoms turns golden, about 2 minutes. Carefully flip and fry until the chicken is golden and cooked through, 1 to 1½ minutes longer. Transfer to a cooling rack or a paper towel–lined plate to drain and season with a pinch of salt.

Let the chicken thighs rest while you build and bake the pizza, then slice into ½-inch-thick slices just before finishing the pizza.

CONTINUED

PIZZA

½ cup (120 g) White Sauce (page 50)

One 10-by-14-inch dough of your choice, in the pan, proofed, and ready to use

1¾ cups (212 g) shredded medium cheddar

4½ cups (510 g) cubed whole-milk low-moisture mozzarella

2 tablespoons (30 g) pickled jalapeños (see page 71, or use store-bought)

2 tablespoons (32 g) Szechuan Chile Oil (page 70)

FOR THE TOP (AFTER BAKING)

3 tablespoons (45 g) mayonnaise

1 teaspoon (15 g) distilled white vinegar or rice vinegar

A few drops (about ⅛ teaspoon) toasted sesame oil

2 tablespoons (30 g) pickled red onions (see page 71, or use store-bought)

1 tablespoon (8 g) thinly sliced scallions

TO BUILD THE PIZZA

Arrange a rack at the bottom of your oven.

Preheat the oven to 550°F (or as hot as it goes).

Use a ladle or spoon to spread the White Sauce across the whole pie, going all the way to the edge.

Along the edges of the pan containing the dough, carefully sprinkle the cheddar in a tight collar to form a 1-inch border.

Working from the outside in, sprinkle the mozzarella over the cheddar and sauce. The cheddar will peep through a bit; the mozzarella should be distributed across the pie.

Sprinkle the pickled jalapeños over the top of the cheese.

Drizzle the Szechuan Chile Oil over the top of the pie.

Bake the pizza for 15 to 18 minutes, or until the bottom of the crust is a deep golden brown and the edges of the pie are crispy.

If you want the top of the pizza to be a bit browner, turn on the broiler and cook the pizza beneath it for a minute or so, just until the cheese starts to bubble and brown in spots.

When the pizza is cooked, remove it from the oven and transfer carefully to a cooling rack. Let cool for 2 to 3 minutes, then transfer to a cutting board and cut into squares.

TO FINISH THE TOP

While the pizza cools, whisk together the mayonnaise, vinegar, and sesame oil.

Top the pie with the sliced chicken and pickled onions.

Drizzle the mayonnaise mixture across the top of the pie, then finish with the scallions. Serve immediately.

KING'S PIE

Top Chef **winner Melissa King helped us develop this salty-sweet pie. Roasted mushrooms give it an earthy, umami base, crispy cups of pepperoni add crunch and spice, and a drizzle of Szechuan-chile honey ties the whole thing together with fiery sweetness. Add a shower of cheese at the end and you've got a pizza that eats like a full-on chef's tasting menu.**

YIELD: ONE 10-BY-14-INCH DETROIT-STYLE PIZZA

ROASTED MUSHROOMS

1¼ cups (159 g) diced mixed mushrooms (brown and king oyster)

1 tablespoon (14 g) extra-virgin olive oil

½ teaspoon (1.5 g) Diamond Crystal kosher salt (see the salt conversion table on page 21 if using other salt)

¼ teaspoon (1 g) freshly ground black pepper

Small pinch of dried thyme

PIZZA

⅔ cup (167 g) Red Sauce (page 46)

One 10-by-14-inch dough of your choice, in the pan, proofed, and ready to use

1¾ cups (212 g) shredded medium cheddar

2¼ cups (240 g) shredded or cubed whole-milk low-moisture mozzarella

2 tablespoons (30 g) chopped pickled peppers (see page 71, or use store-bought, like Mama Lil's)

35 slices (60 g) cup-and-char pepperoni

FOR THE TOP (AFTER BAKING)

2 tablespoons (16 g) freshly grated Grana Padano or Parmesan

4 tablespoons (60 g) Hot Honey, made with Szechuan peppercorns (see page 67 for guidance)

TO PREPARE THE MUSHROOMS

Arrange a rack at the bottom of your oven.

Preheat the oven to 550°F (or as high as it goes).

In a small mixing bowl, combine the mushrooms, oil, salt, pepper, and thyme.

Spread the mushrooms in an even layer in a small roasting dish or oven-safe frying pan and roast for 8 to 10 minutes, stirring once, until nicely browned. Let them cool until ready to build the pizza.

TO BUILD THE PIZZA

Ladle or spoon the Red Sauce over the pie, going all the way to the edge, and use the back of the ladle or spoon to gently spread it into a thin, even layer.

Along the edges of the pan containing the dough, carefully sprinkle the cheddar in a tight collar to form a 1-inch border.

Working from the outside in, sprinkle the low-moisture mozzarella over the cheddar and sauce. The cheddar and sauce will peep through a bit; the mozzarella should be distributed across the pie.

Sprinkle the cooked mushrooms and the chopped pickled peppers across the cheese. Carefully arrange the pepperoni in five rows of seven. Bake the pizza for 15 to 18 minutes, or until the bottom of the crust is a deep golden brown and the edges of the pie are crispy.

When the pizza is cooked, remove it from the oven and transfer carefully to a cooling rack. Let cool for 2 to 3 minutes, then transfer to a cutting board and cut into squares.

TO FINISH THE TOP

Top with the Grana Padano and drizzle with the Szechuan Hot Honey and serve immediately.

BUFFALO CHICKEN PIE

This pizza is absolutely brimming with Buffalo sauce flavor. It's a triple threat: spicy roasted chicken, buttery Buffalo-Tomato Sauce, and creamy Buffalo Dip. Sure, it's a bit of a project, but, when you think about it, it's basically three game-day snacks in one: wings, pizza, and dip. Serve it with cold drinks and loud friends.

YIELD: ONE 10-BY-14-INCH DETROIT-STYLE PIZZA

BUFFALO CHICKEN

2 boneless, skinless chicken thighs (about 8 ounces or 240 g)

1 tablespoon (14 g) extra-virgin olive oil

½ teaspoon (1.5 g) Diamond Crystal salt (see the salt conversion table on page 21 if using other salt)

2 tablespoons (32 g) cayenne-based hot sauce, such as Crystal or Tabasco

4 tablespoons (57 g) unsalted butter, melted

BUFFALO TOMATO SAUCE

2 tablespoons (32 g) cayenne-based hot sauce, such as Crystal or Tabasco

4 tablespoons (57 g) unsalted butter, melted

⅓ cup (80 g) canned crushed tomatoes

¼ teaspoon (0.7 g) Diamond Crystal kosher salt (see the salt conversion table on page 21 if using other salt)

TO PREPARE THE CHICKEN

Preheat the oven to 450°F.

Place the chicken thighs on a rimmed baking sheet and drizzle with the oil.

Use clean hands to rub the oil all over the thighs.

Sprinkle the thighs with the salt and arrange on the baking sheet.

Roast the thighs for 18 to 20 minutes, until an internal thermometer registers at least 160°F.

While the chicken roasts, stir the hot sauce and butter together in a small bowl.

Once the chicken is finished cooking, let it rest for 10 minutes, then chop the meat into 1-inch pieces.

Gently toss the chicken with the hot sauce–butter mixture and let sit until you're ready to build the pizza.

TO PREPARE THE BUFFALO TOMATO SAUCE

Stir the ingredients together in a small bowl and let sit until you're ready to build the pizza.

CONTINUED

BUFFALO DIP

¼ cup (61 g) cream cheese, softened

6 tablespoons (92 g) heavy cream

6 tablespoons (92 g) ranch dressing

3 tablespoons (48 g) hot sauce

1 tablespoon (15 g) white vinegar

2 cloves garlic (about 6 g), minced

2 tablespoons (16 g) thinly sliced scallions

PIZZA

One 10-by-14-inch dough of your choice, in the pan, proofed, and ready to use

1¾ cups (212 g) shredded medium cheddar

2¼ cups (240 g) shredded or cubed whole-milk low-moisture mozzarella

FOR THE TOP (AFTER BAKING)

3 tablespoons (45 g) House Ranch (page 64) mixed with 1 to 2 teaspoons (5 to 10 g) vinegar-based hot sauce (or reserved Buffalo Dip)

2 tablespoons (16 g) thinly sliced scallions

TO PREPARE THE BUFFALO DIP

Stir the ingredients together in a medium bowl and let sit until you are ready to build the pizza.

TO BUILD THE PIZZA

Arrange a rack at the bottom of your oven.

Preheat the oven to 550°F (or as hot as your oven allows).

Ladle or spoon the Buffalo Tomato Sauce across the whole pie, and use the back of the ladle or spoon to gently spread it into a thin, even layer.

Along the edges of the pan containing the dough, carefully sprinkle the cheddar in a tight collar to form a 1-inch border.

Use a spoon or rubber scraper spatula to spread the Buffalo Dip across the entire pie, from edge to edge.

Working from the outside in, sprinkle the mozzarella over the Buffalo Dip. The dip will peep through a bit; the mozzarella should be distributed across the pie.

Distribute the chicken evenly across the cheese.

Bake the pizza for 15 to 18 minutes, or until the bottom of the crust is a deep golden brown and the edges of the pie are crispy.

When the pizza is cooked, remove it from the oven and transfer carefully to a cooling rack. Let cool for 2 to 3 minutes, then transfer to a cutting board and cut into squares

TO FINISH THE TOP

Drizzle the pie with the Buffalo Ranch, sprinkle with the sliced scallions, and serve immediately.

VEGGIE PIE GUY

An all-vegetable pizza can be glorious, but too often it's soggy and overloaded due to watery mushrooms and a salad bar's worth of raw vegetables. This minimalist approach, however, uses sautéed onions, crispy kale, Garlic Confit, and pickled peppers, avoiding excess moisture and highlighting flavors beautifully. Vibrant Sun-Dried Tomato Vinaigrette adds brightness and a bit of sweetness. We like to customize this pie seasonally at the restaurant. Just remember, less is more.

YIELD: ONE 10-BY-14-INCH DETROIT-STYLE PIZZA

ONIONS

1 tablespoon (14 g) extra-virgin olive oil

2 medium onions (255 g), chopped

¼ teaspoon (0.7 g) Diamond Crystal kosher salt (see the salt conversion table on page 21 if using other salt)

PIZZA

¾ cup (180 g) Red Sauce (page 46)

One 10-by-14-inch dough of your choice, in the pan, proofed, and ready to use

1¾ cups (212 g) shredded medium cheddar

6 cups (179 g) loosely packed baby kale or thinly sliced dinosaur kale

2⅛ cups (240 g) shredded or cubed whole-milk low-moisture mozzarella cheese

2 tablespoons (30 g) chopped pickled peppers (see page 71, or use store-bought, like Mama Lil's)

4 tablespoons (121 g) Garlic Confit (page 60), drained

FOR THE TOP (AFTER BAKING)

4 tablespoons (61 g) Sun-Dried Tomato Vinaigrette (page 54)

TO PREPARE THE ONIONS

Heat a large, heavy-bottomed frying pan over medium heat. Add the olive oil and onions, then cook for 5 to 7 minutes, stirring occasionally, until the onions begin to turn golden brown. Sprinkle with the salt, stir gently to combine, and transfer to a bowl until ready to build the pizza.

TO BUILD THE PIZZA

Arrange a rack at the bottom of your oven. Preheat the oven to 550°F (or as hot as your oven allows).

Spread the Red Sauce in a thin, even layer. Sprinkle the cooked onions and kale evenly across the pie from end to end. Along the edges of the pan containing the dough, sprinkle the cheddar in a tight collar to form a 1-inch border.

Working from the outside in, sprinkle the mozzarella over the cheddar, sauce, onions, and kale. The toppings will peep through a bit. Sprinkle the chopped pickled peppers and Garlic Confit evenly over the cheese.

Bake for 15 to 18 minutes, or until the bottom of the crust is a deep golden brown and the edges are crispy.

For a browner top, broil for about a minute until the cheese bubbles and browns (watch carefully to avoid overcooking the kale).

When the pizza is cooked, remove it from the oven and transfer carefully to a cooling rack. Let cool for 2 to 3 minutes.

TO FINISH THE TOP

Drizzle the pie with the Sun-Dried Tomato Vinaigrette.

Cut into squares and serve immediately.

DA GRUBBY

Bold, messy, and ridiculous—in the best way. Named for Bay Area–based food influencer GrubWitMike, Da Grubby is our homage to late-night eats: juicy gochujang BBQ chicken, garlicky ricotta, and a drizzle of Alabama White Sauce. It's smoky, spicy, and loud, just like a good night out with your friends. Crisp scallions and sesame seeds add freshness and crunch. Don't even try to eat this one neatly.

YIELD: ONE 10-BY-14-INCH DETROIT-STYLE PIZZA

CHICKEN

2 boneless, skinless chicken thighs (about 8 ounces or 240 g)

2 tablespoons (28 g) extra-virgin olive oil, divided

1 teaspoon (3 g) kosher salt (see the salt conversion table on page 21 if using other salt)

½ teaspoon (3 g) dried oregano

2 cloves garlic (about 6 g), minced

Zest and juice of ½ medium lemon (about 1½ tablespoons or 23 g juice)

½ teaspoon (1 g) black pepper

4 tablespoons (60 g) SPG BBQ Sauce (page 69)

1 tablespoon gochujang

PIZZA

Juice of ½ medium lemon (about 1½ tablespoons or 23 g juice)

½ cup (120 g) White Sauce (page 50)

One 10-by-14-inch dough of your choice, in the pan, proofed, and ready to use

1¾ cups (212 g) shredded medium cheddar

2¼ cups (240 g) cubed whole-milk low-moisture mozzarella

4 tablespoons (60 g) pickled Fresno chiles (see page 71, or use store-bought)

TO PREPARE THE CHICKEN

Move an oven rack to the bottom position and preheat the oven to 450°F.

Place the chicken thighs on a rimmed baking sheet and drizzle with 1 tablespoon (14 g) of the olive oil.

Use clean hands to rub the oil all over the thighs.

Sprinkle the thighs with the salt and arrange on the baking sheet.

Roast the thighs for 18 to 20 minutes, until an internal thermometer registers at least 160°F.

While the chicken roasts, whisk together the remaining 1 tablespoon (14 g) of oil, oregano, garlic, lemon zest and juice, and black pepper in a small bowl.

In another small bowl, whisk together the SPG BBQ Sauce and the gochujang.

Once the chicken is finished cooking, let it rest for 10 minutes, then chop the meat into 1-inch pieces.

Toss the chicken with the gochujang BBQ Sauce and let sit until ready to prepare the pizza.

ALABAMA WHITE SAUCE

3 tablespoons (45 g) mayonnaise

1½ teaspoons (8 g) Worcestershire sauce

2 teaspoons (15 g) Hot Honey (page 67)

1 teaspoon (5 g) Dijon mustard

1 teaspoon (5 g) pickle brine or distilled white vinegar

1 teaspoon (5 g) liquid from pickled Fresnos (not the solids)

1 clove garlic, finely chopped (about 3 g)

¼ teaspoon (0.7g) Diamond Crystal kosher salt (see the salt conversion table on page 21 if using other salt)

¼ teaspoon (1 g) black pepper

FOR THE TOP (AFTER BAKING)

2 tablespoons (16 g) thinly sliced scallions

1 tablespoon (11 g) toasted sesame seeds

TO BUILD THE PIZZA

Arrange a rack at the bottom of your oven. Preheat the oven to 550°F (or as hot as your oven allows).

In a small bowl, stir the lemon juice into the White Sauce and spread it across the top of the dough, going all the way to the edge of the pie in a thin, even layer using the back of a spoon.

Along the edges of the pan containing the dough, carefully sprinkle the cheddar in a tight collar to form a 1-inch border.

Working from the outside in, sprinkle the mozzarella over the cheddar and sauce. The cheddar will peep through a bit; the mozzarella should be distributed across the pie.

Distribute the pickled Fresno slices evenly across the pizza.

Scatter the chicken evenly over the top.

Bake for 14 to 18 minutes, or until the bottom is deeply golden and the cheese is bubbling and browned in spots.

Take the pizza out of the oven and transfer to a cooling rack for 2 to 3 minutes, then transfer to a cutting board and cut into squares.

TO MAKE THE ALABAMA WHITE SAUCE

While the pizza cools, whisk the Alabama White Sauce ingredients together and set aside.

Drizzle the Alabama White Sauce over the top of the cut pizza.

TO FINISH THE TOP

Sprinkle with the chopped scallions and toasted sesame seeds and serve immediately.

CHICKEN TIKKA-ISH

This riff on chicken tikka masala was the brainchild of our former director of marketing and innovation, Priya Kane, and chef and cookbook author Hetal Vasavada, aka *Milk and Cardamom*. A creamy tomato sauce, tandoori-spiced chicken, garam masala, and Kashmiri chile paste build deep, warming heat and bring bold Indian flavors. A cilantro-mint drizzle and tangy pickled onions balance it all out. It's not traditional, but it is delicious. Great with a cold beer or mango lassi.

YIELD: ONE 10-BY-14-INCH DETROIT-STYLE PIZZA

MASALA PICKLED ONIONS

2 tablespoons (30 g) pickled red onions (see page 71, or use store-bought), drained

Pinch of ground cumin

Pinch of ground coriander

Pinch of Kashmiri chile powder

CILANTRO-MINT YOGURT

¼ cup (60 g) Greek yogurt

2 tablespoons (4 g) roughly chopped fresh cilantro, tender stems okay

1 tablespoon (1 g) fresh mint leaves

1 teaspoon (2 g) lemon juice

½ teaspoon (1 g) chopped garlic

¼ teaspoon (0.5 g) ground cumin

Small pinch of ground cinnamon

¼ teaspoon (0.7 g) Diamond Crystal kosher salt (see the salt conversion chart on page 21 if using other salt)

½ small serrano chile (or to taste), stemmed and chopped

TANDOORI MASALA PASTE

½ teaspoon (2 g) black pepper

1 tablespoon (10 g) garam masala

½ teaspoon (2 g) turmeric

2 teaspoons (6 g) Diamond Crystal kosher salt (see the salt conversion chart on page 21 if using other salt)

1 tablespoon (16 g) Kashmiri chile powder

TO MAKE THE MASALA PICKLED ONIONS

Use your hands or a spoon to thoroughly combine the ingredients in a bowl. Refrigerate until ready to use.

TO MAKE THE CILANTRO-MINT YOGURT

Combine all the ingredients in a food processor or blender. Taste and adjust the seasoning as needed. Refrigerate until ready to use.

TO MAKE THE TANDOORI MASALA PASTE

In a medium mixing bowl, combine the black pepper, garam masala, turmeric, kosher salt, chile powder, fenugreek, and paprika. Stir well to blend the spices evenly.

Add the olive oil, garlic, lemon juice, ginger, and Greek yogurt.

Whisk the mixture until a smooth, thick paste forms.

TO MAKE THE TANDOORI CHICKEN

In a medium bowl, combine the chicken thighs with the olive oil, salt, and half of the Tandoori Masala Paste. Use your hands or a spoon to coat evenly.

Cover and marinate in the refrigerator for at least 4 hours, or preferably overnight.

Preheat your oven to 450°F. Line a rimmed sheet tray or baking dish with foil or parchment.

Arrange the chicken thighs on the sheet tray and roast for 18 to 22 minutes, until cooked through and starting to brown on the edges. The internal temperature should reach 165°F.

Let cool for 5 to 10 minutes, then dice the chicken into ½-inch pieces.

CONTINUED

¼ teaspoon (3 g) ground fenugreek

½ teaspoon (2 g) paprika

4 tablespoons (64 g) olive oil

4 cloves garlic (about 13 g), minced

3 tablespoons (about 48 g) lemon juice (juice of 1 lemon)

1 tablespoon (19 g) grated fresh ginger

½ cup (128 g) Greek yogurt

TANDOORI CHICKEN

3 boneless, skinless chicken thighs (about 12 ounces or 360 g)

1 teaspoon (5 g) extra-virgin olive oil

1 teaspoon (3 g) Diamond Crystal kosher salt (see the salt conversion chart on page 21 if using other salt)

TIKKA MASALA SAUCE

1 tablespoon (14 g) olive oil

1 medium yellow onion (about 150 g), chopped

¼ teaspoon (0.7 g) Diamond Crystal kosher salt (see the salt conversion chart on page 21 if using other salt)

¾ cup (170 g) canned, crushed tomatoes

1 tablespoon (13 g) sugar

4 tablespoons (64 g) heavy cream

PIZZA

One 10-by-14-inch dough of your choice, in the pan, proofed, and ready to use

1⅔ cups (212 g) shredded medium cheddar

2¼ cups (240 g) shredded or diced whole-milk low-moisture mozzarella

FOR THE TOP (AFTER BAKING)

2 tablespoons (16 g) thinly sliced scallions

Use immediately, or store in an airtight container in the refrigerator for up to 4 days

TO MAKE THE TIKKA MASALA SAUCE

In a medium saucepan, heat the olive oil over medium heat, then sauté the onions for 4 to 5 minutes until fragrant. Season with the salt.

Add the remaining half of the Tandoori Masala Paste and sauté until fragrant, 1 to 2 minutes. Then add the crushed tomatoes and sugar and stir well. Cook for 6 to 7 minutes, until it begins to thicken, then stir in the heavy cream and remove from the heat. Let cool before building the pizza.

TO BUILD THE PIZZA

Arrange a rack at the bottom of your oven.

Preheat the oven to 550°F (or as hot as your oven allows).

Spread the Tikka Masala Sauce evenly across the whole pie, going all the way to the edge.

Along the edges of the pan containing the dough, carefully sprinkle the cheddar to form a tight 1-inch border.

Add the mozzarella to the center of the pizza and gently spread it into an even layer using clean hands. The sauce should peek through in spots.

Scatter the diced tandoori chicken evenly across the pizza.

Bake for 15 to 18 minutes, or until the crust is golden and the cheese is bubbling and starting to brown.

Transfer to a cooling rack and let cool for 2 to 3 minutes, then transfer to a cutting board and cut into squares.

TO FINISH THE TOP

Garnish the pizza with the Masala Pickled Onions, Cilantro-Mint Yogurt, and chopped scallions. Serve immediately.

NOTE: IN THE RESTAURANT, WE PARTNERED WITH SACH FOODS TO MAKE A PHENOMENAL VEGETARIAN VERSION OF THIS PIE USING THEIR PANEER. TO MAKE IT, MARINATE CUBED PANEER IN PLACE OF THE CHICKEN. MARINATE IT IN THE TANDOORI MASALA PASTE AND BROIL IT UNTIL NICELY CHARRED.

BIG VON

Named for Bay Area radio legend Big Von, who was one of our first customers and who custom-ordered this combo on the regular, this pie upgrades a classic sausage-and-pepperoni combo with a garlicky White Sauce and Hot Honey. The crispy pepperoni cups hold spicy honey pools perfectly. It's rooted in classic flavors, but still a little offbeat—a pie that will please pizza purists and adventurers alike.

YIELD: ONE 10-BY-14-INCH DETROIT-STYLE PIZZA

PIZZA

¾ cup (180 g) White Sauce (page 50)

One 10-by-14-inch dough of your choice, in the pan, proofed, and ready to use

1¾ cups (212 g) shredded medium cheddar

8 ounces (240 g) mild Italian sausage, casing removed, cut into 1-inch pieces

2¼ cups (240 g) shredded or cubed whole-milk low-moisture mozzarella

60 slices (105 g) cup-and-char pepperoni

FOR THE TOP (AFTER BAKING)

4 tablespoons (61 g) Hot Honey (page 67)

TO BUILD THE PIZZA

Arrange a rack at the bottom of your oven.

Preheat the oven to 550°F (or as hot as it goes).

Ladle or spoon the White Sauce across the top of the pie and use the back of the ladle or spoon to gently spread it into a thin, even layer.

Along the edges of the pan containing the dough, carefully sprinkle the cheddar in a tight collar to form a 1-inch border.

Distribute the sausage evenly across the pie, making sure to cover it from edge to edge.

Working from the outside in, sprinkle the low-moisture mozzarella over the cheddar, sauce, and sausage. The other ingredients will peep through a bit; the mozzarella should be distributed across the pie.

Arrange the pepperoni across the mozzarella in 6 rows of 10.

Bake the pizza for 15 to 18 minutes, or until the bottom of the crust is a deep golden brown and the edges of the pie are crispy.

If you want the top of the pizza to be a bit browner, turn on the broiler and cook the pizza beneath it for a minute or so, just until the cheese starts to bubble and brown in spots.

When the pizza is cooked, remove it from the oven and transfer carefully to a cooling rack. Let cool for 2 to 3 minutes, then transfer to a cutting board and cut into squares.

TO FINISH THE TOP

Drizzle the pie with the Hot Honey and serve immediately.

OUT OF THE BOX

Introduction

You won't ever catch me without at least one batch of prepared pizza dough in my refrigerator, and it isn't only because I sling it for a living. Pizza dough happens to be just about the easiest yeasted dough on the planet, and the most versatile, too. This chapter is your permission slip to start thinking about dough beyond the pizza pan.

With its high hydration and slow fermentation, Detroit-style dough isn't just good for the square pies in the last two chapters—it's a springboard for all kinds of bready brilliance. We're talking golden-edged focaccia, airy ciabatta, gooey pull-apart cheesy bread, sticky monkey bread, and even doughnuts that toe the line between breakfast and "Is this dessert?" And the best part? You already did the "hard" part by mixing and kneading. Now it's time to play.

One of the most magical things about the doughs in this book is their structure: The high water content gives them a tender, open crumb and a beautifully chewy bite, while their slow rise develops flavor and elasticity that makes them super versatile. This is the kind of dough that plays well with others—slather it with garlic butter, dunk it in cinnamon sugar, stuff it with cheese, or just tear off hunks to dip in olive oil. Because you're not relying on it to hold sauce and toppings anymore, you can stretch it a little thinner, bake it a little hotter, or get weird with it in the best possible way.

So consider this chapter your edible backup plan. Make a double batch of dough and turn one half into a Detroit-style pie, but roll the second one into a ball and let it hang out in your fridge for a couple of days. The next time hunger strikes, you'll have a built-in solution for last-minute bread, an emergency brunch hero move, or an improvised dessert. These recipes are less about precision and more about possibility. You've already nailed the base—now let's get a little weird with it.

ONE NOTE ABOUT USING GLUTEN-FREE DOUGH:

Some of the recipes in this chapter won't work with the **GLUTEN-FREE DOUGH** as the recipe is written, because that dough is so wet and batter-like. (Those that will work are noted as such.) To make the GF dough easier to work with, **MIX 2 TABLESPOONS (ABOUT 10 G) WHOLE PSYLLIUM HUSKS** into the water before you add it to the dough. Stir well and **LET IT SIT FOR ABOUT A MINUTE**, until it turns into a **THICK GEL-LIKE SUBSTANCE**, then follow the rest of the recipe as written. You'll end up with a gluten-free dough that may be **EASILY SHAPED OR ROLLED**, as called for in these recipes. It can't be hand-stretched, as in the New York–Style Pie (page 135), but a **GOOD ROLLING PIN** will get the job done just fine.

CIABATTA ROLLS

This is one of the easiest ways to turn leftover pizza dough into something totally new. With a quick pre-shape and a couple of short proofing periods, you'll end up with crusty, airy rolls perfect for sandwiches or soaking up sauce. The key is handling the dough gently so you preserve those gorgeous air bubbles. Bonus: Your kitchen will smell like a bakery.

YIELD: 4 TO 6 ROLLS (DEPENDING ON SIZE)

All-purpose flour for dusting

1 recipe (about 560 g) pizza dough of your choice (if you're using Gluten-Free Dough, see the note about it in the introduction to this chapter, page 129)

Lightly flour a work surface and gently turn out the pizza dough. Dust the top with a little more flour and gently stretch into a rectangle about 6 by 8 inches.

Cover the dough with a clean towel and let rest for 20 to 30 minutes, until slightly puffed and relaxed.

Using a bench scraper or sharp knife, cut the dough into 4 to 6 rectangular pieces (depending on desired roll size). Handle carefully to preserve the air bubbles.

Transfer the pieces to a parchment-lined baking sheet, spacing them slightly apart. Cover loosely with plastic or a damp towel and let rise for another 30 to 45 minutes, until puffy but not doubled.

While the rolls are rising, preheat the oven to 475°F. Place a metal pan on the bottom rack; it will be used during baking to create steam.

Just before baking, dust the tops lightly with flour. Place the tray on the middle rack and add 1 cup (240 g) of hot water to the bottom pan to generate steam. Bake for 20 to 25 minutes, until golden and crisp.

Transfer the rolls to a wire rack and let cool completely before slicing.

HOUSE FOCACCIA

With a dimpled surface, crispy edges, and a topping of garlicky oil, cheese, and herbs, this bread turns a humble base into something luxurious. It's great on its own, sliced for sandwiches, or torn into chunks for dipping. Don't skip the full cooling time—it helps lock in that crisp-chewy texture.

YIELD: ONE 10-BY-14-INCH FOCACCIA LOAF

2 tablespoons (28 g) extra-virgin olive oil (or use the oil from Garlic Confit, page 60)

1 teaspoon (3 g) garlic powder

One 10-by-14-inch dough of your choice, in the pan, proofed (but not parbaked), and ready to use (Gluten-Free Dough works as written here)

1½ ounces (43 g) Grana Padano or Parmesan, grated

Pinch of dried oregano

Preheat the oven to 550°F (or as high as it allows).

In a small bowl, mix the extra-virgin olive oil with the garlic powder (omit these if using oil from the Garlic Confit).

Brush the olive oil evenly across the surface of the dough. Sprinkle the grated cheese and oregano evenly over the top.

Bake for 15 to 18 minutes, or until the focaccia is golden and crisped at the edges.

Immediately turn the baked focaccia out onto a wire cooling rack. Allow it to cool fully at room temperature (about 2 hours). Do not slice while warm.

NEW YORK–STYLE PIE

A classic NYC-style cheese pizza is all about simplicity—just dough, sauce, cheese, and a hot oven. This version uses the same high-hydration dough you've been working with all along, proving it's not just for the pan. Grab your pizza stone (or a flipped baking sheet) and let's make it happen.

YIELD: ONE 10- TO 12-INCH PIZZA

All-purpose flour or semolina for dusting

½ recipe (about 280 g) pizza dough of your choice, at room temperature (if you're using Gluten-Free Dough, see the note about it in the introduction to this chapter, page 129)

¼ cup (60 g) Red Sauce (page 46)

¾ cup (85 g) shredded whole-milk low-moisture mozzarella

1 ounce (30 g) whole-milk fresh mozzarella, torn into 1-inch chunks

Place a pizza stone on the center rack of your oven and preheat to 550°F (or as hot as your oven allows) for at least 45 minutes. No stone? Use an upside-down baking sheet—just make sure it preheats along with the oven.

On a lightly floured surface, stretch the dough into a 10- to 12-inch round. Try not to deflate the edges—you want those puffy crust bubbles.

Transfer the dough to a lightly floured (or semolina-dusted) pizza peel or cutting board. Spread the Red Sauce evenly over the base, leaving about a ½-inch border. Top with the cheeses.

Slide the pizza onto the hot stone or sheet and bake for 6 to 8 minutes, or until the crust is puffed and browned and the cheese is bubbling and just starting to brown.

Remove from the oven, let it sit for a minute (if you can wait), then slice and serve.

GARLIC CHEESY BREAD

This is what happens when pizza dough and garlic bread have a baby. It's got all the cheese, crunch, and golden-brown edges you want in a pizza, finished with just enough garlic sharpness. The bread is deliciously indulgent as it is, but dunking it in your favorite sauce pushes it over the top and you'll never want it any other way.

YIELD: ONE 10-BY-14-INCH CHEESY BREAD

GARLIC OIL

1 tablespoon (14 g) extra-virgin olive oil

1 clove garlic (about 3 g), smashed with the back of a knife

CHEESY BREAD

One 10-by-14-inch dough of your choice, in the pan proofed, and ready to use (Gluten-Free Dough works as written here)

1⅓ cups (212 g) shredded medium cheddar

2¼ cups (240 g) shredded or diced whole-milk low-moisture mozzarella

FOR THE TOP (AFTER BAKING)

3 tablespoons (28 g) freshly grated Parmesan or Grana Padano

2 tablespoons (about 16 g) fresh parsley leaves, finely chopped

FOR DIPPING

Red Sauce (page 46), Fresh Herb Pesto (page 61), House Ranch (page 64), or sauce of your choice

TO MAKE THE GARLIC OIL

Combine the ingredients in a small bowl and set aside while you build and bake the bread.

TO BUILD THE CHEESY BREAD

Arrange a rack at the bottom of your oven.

Preheat the oven to 550°F (or as hot as it goes).

Along the edges of the pan containing the dough, carefully sprinkle the cheddar in a tight collar to form a 1-inch border.

Working from the outside in, sprinkle the low-moisture mozzarella over the whole pie, going all the way to the edge. The cheddar will peep through a bit; the mozzarella should be distributed across the pie.

Bake for 15 to 18 minutes, or until the bottom of the crust is a deep golden brown and the edges of the pie are crispy.

If you want the top to be a bit browner, turn on the broiler and cook the bread beneath it for a minute or so, just until the cheese starts to bubble and brown in spots.

When the bread is cooked, remove it from the oven and transfer carefully to a cooling rack. Let cool for 2 to 3 minutes, then transfer to a cutting board and cut into squares.

TO FINISH THE TOP

Remove the garlic clove from the garlic oil and drizzle the infused oil over the top of the bread. Sprinkle the grated Parmesan and fresh parsley across the pie, and serve immediately with your dipping sauce of choice.

VODKA CHICKEN PARM SANDWICHES

These sandwiches hit every nostalgic note—crispy chicken, melty cheese, and slightly spicy, thanks to the Vodka Sauce. They're perfect for a dinner party or wrapped in foil and eaten al fresco in your favorite park. They're best served just after assembling, but don't be surprised if you find yourself sneaking one cold out of the fridge the next day—they're that good.

YIELD: 4 SANDWICHES

HOMEMADE CHICKEN CUTLETS

2 boneless, skinless chicken breasts (about 1 pound or 450 g)

Salt and black pepper

½ cup (65 g) all-purpose flour

2 large eggs, beaten

1 cup (100 g) breadcrumbs (Italian-style or plain with added herbs)

½ cup (45 g) grated Parmesan

Neutral oil for frying (about ¼ cup [56 g] depending on the size of your pan)

PESTO AIOLI

¼ cup (60 g) mayonnaise

¼ cup (60 g) Fresh Herb Pesto (page 61)

Juice of ½ lemon (about 1½ tablespoons or 23 g)

TO MAKE THE CHICKEN CUTLETS

Slice each chicken breast in half horizontally to make four thin cutlets.

Season the cutlets with salt and pepper to taste.

Arrange the flour, the beaten eggs, and the breadcrumbs combined with the grated cheese in three separate wide, shallow bowls or large plates.

Dredge each piece in the flour, dip into the beaten eggs, then coat in a mixture of the breadcrumbs and Parmesan.

Heat ¼ inch of oil in a skillet over medium heat. Fry the cutlets for 2 to 3 minutes per side, or until golden and cooked through. Drain on a rack or paper towels.

TO MAKE THE PESTO AIOLI

In a small bowl, stir together the mayonnaise, pesto, and lemon juice. Refrigerate until ready to use.

CONTINUED

SANDWICHES

- ¾ cup (180 g) Vodka Sauce (page 49)
- 1 loaf House Focaccia (page 132), baked and cooled, cut into 4 sandwich-size portions and halved horizontally, or 4 Ciabatta Rolls (page 131), halved lengthwise, or 4 large, crusty sandwich rolls of your choice
- 8 slices (about 200 g) whole-milk low-moisture mozzarella
- 4 tablespoons (24 g) grated Grana Padano or Parmesan
- 4 small pinches of dried oregano
- 8 to 12 fresh basil leaves

TO ASSEMBLE THE SANDWICHES

In a small pot, warm the Vodka Sauce over low heat. Keep covered and simmering until ready to use.

Place the bottom halves of the focaccia cut-side up on a sheet pan.

Spread about 1 tablespoon (14 g) of warm Vodka Sauce on each piece.

Top each with a chicken cutlet.

Spoon about 3 tablespoons (45 g) of warm Vodka Sauce over each cutlet.

Top with 2 slices of mozzarella, 1 tablespoon (6 g) of Grana Padano, and a pinch of oregano.

Top each sandwich with the remaining focaccia pieces.

TO BAKE AND FINISH

Preheat the oven to 450°F.

Bake the sandwiches for 5 to 7 minutes, or until the cheese is melted and the sandwich is heated through.

Remove from the oven. Open each sandwich slightly and add 2 or 3 basil leaves on top of the melted cheese.

Spread 1 to 2 tablespoons (14 to 28 g) of the Pesto Aioli on the top piece of bread.

Close, cut in half with a serrated knife if desired, and serve hot.

root

APPLE CARAMEL MONKEY BREAD

This dessert feels like a cozy fall evening in carb form. Roasted apples, cinnamon sugar, and buttery pizza dough come together into a gooey, caramelized pull-apart masterpiece. It's easy to make, wildly satisfying, and even better eaten with your fingers. Serve warm for maximum ooze factor.

YIELD: 4 SERVINGS

ROASTED APPLES

2 large apples (about 400 g), such as Honeycrisp, Fuji, or Granny Smith, peeled, cored, and diced

1 tablespoon (14 g) unsalted butter, melted

1 tablespoon (12 g) light brown sugar

1 tablespoon (12 g) granulated sugar

¼ teaspoon (1 g) ground cinnamon

Pinch of Diamond Crystal kosher salt (see the salt conversion table on page 21 if using other salt)

1 teaspoon (5 g) fresh lemon juice

SUGAR COATING AND PAN BASE

4 tablespoons (50 g) light brown sugar

4 tablespoons (50 g) granulated sugar

1 teaspoon (3 g) ground cinnamon

¼ teaspoon (0.7 g) Diamond Crystal kosher salt (see the salt conversion table on page 21 if using other salt)

5 tablespoons (71 g) unsalted butter, melted and divided

DOUGH

All-purpose flour for dusting

1 pound (450 g) pizza dough of your choice (if you're using Gluten-Free Dough, see the note about it in the introduction to this chapter, page 129)

TO PREPARE THE ROASTED APPLES

Preheat the oven to 375°F.

In a medium baking dish, toss the diced apple with the butter, sugars, cinnamon, salt, and lemon juice.

Roast for 20 to 25 minutes, stirring once halfway through, until the apples are soft, bubbling, and slightly caramelized. Set aside to cool slightly. Leave the oven on but reduce the heat to 350°F.

TO PREPARE THE SUGAR COATING AND PAN BASE

In a small bowl, mix the sugars, cinnamon, and salt.

Lightly brush an 8-by-8-inch square baking dish with 2 tablespoons (28 g) of the melted butter and sprinkle it with half the cinnamon-sugar mixture.

TO PREPARE THE DOUGH

On a lightly floured surface, use your hands to roll the pizza dough into an 8-inch log.

Use a sharp knife to slice the log in half lengthwise, then cut each half into 8 equal pieces and roll each one into a ball. You should have 16 dough balls.

Set up a little assembly line with the remaining 3 tablespoons (43 g) of melted butter and the remaining cinnamon-sugar mixture.

Dip each dough ball into the melted butter, then roll it in the sugar mixture until fully coated.

Spread the roasted apple mixture over the sugar base in the pan.

Arrange the 16 coated dough pieces over the apples in a 4-by-4 grid, loosely packed.

Bake for 25 to 30 minutes, or until puffed and golden brown on top. Let cool slightly before inverting onto a plate or serving directly from the pan.

BABKA MONKEY BREAD

This is babka meets pull-apart bread, with swirls of hot fudge and a cinnamon-sugar coating that turns crisp in the oven. Each bite is gooey, sweet, and a little over the top—in the best way. It's a total crowd-pleaser whether you serve it straight from the pan or flipped onto a platter with extra fudge. Breakfast or dessert? You decide.

YIELD: 4 SERVINGS

SUGAR COATING AND PAN BASE

3 tablespoons (43 g) unsalted butter, melted and divided

¼ cup (30 g) light brown sugar

¼ cup (50 g) granulated sugar

1 teaspoon (3 g) ground cinnamon

DOUGH

All-purpose flour for dusting

1 pound (450 g) pizza dough of your choice (if you're using Gluten-Free Dough, see the note about it in the introduction to this chapter, page 129)

½ cup (120 g) Hot Fudge Sauce (page 145), cooled (keep cold in the fridge until ready to assemble the monkey bread), plus more, warmed, for serving (optional)

TO PREPARE THE SUGAR COATING AND PAN BASE

Preheat the oven to 350°F.

Lightly brush a 6-cup loaf pan with 1 tablespoon (14 g) of the melted butter.

In a small bowl, mix together the brown sugar, granulated sugar, and cinnamon. Set aside.

TO PREPARE THE DOUGH

On a lightly floured surface, roll the pizza dough into a long, even log. Cut the log in half, then cut each half into 6 equal pieces—you'll have 12 dough pieces total.

Flatten each piece slightly. Place about 1 teaspoon (5 g) of the chilled fudge sauce in the center of each piece, then pinch the dough closed to seal it into a ball.

Dip all the filled dough balls in the remaining 2 tablespoons (28 g) of melted butter, then roll them in the cinnamon sugar until fully coated.

Sprinkle a few spoonfuls of the remaining cinnamon sugar onto the bottom of the loaf pan. If desired, add a few spoonfuls of extra hot fudge on the base for added gooeyness.

Arrange the 16 filled, coated dough balls in the loaf pan in 2 rows of 8. It's okay if they overlap a bit—they'll bake together into pull-apart layers.

Bake for 25 to 30 minutes, or until the dough is puffed and golden brown and the sugar is bubbling around the edges.

Let the monkey bread cool in the pan for 5 to 10 minutes before inverting onto a plate, or serving warm directly from the pan. Drizzle with extra hot fudge if you'd like and serve warm.

UPSIDE-DOWN STRAWBERRY MONKEY BREAD WITH CREAM CHEESE ICING

Part breakfast, part dessert, all fun—this sticky-sweet monkey bread is baked upside down so all the jammy strawberry goodness lands right on top.

YIELD: 4 SERVINGS

SUGAR COATING AND PAN BASE

4 tablespoons (50 g) light brown sugar

4 tablespoons (50 g) granulated sugar

1 teaspoon (3 g) ground cinnamon

¼ teaspoon (1.5 g) kosher salt (see the salt conversion table on page 21 if using other salt)

5 tablespoons (71 g) unsalted butter, melted and divided

DOUGH

All-purpose flour for dusting

1 pound (450 g) pizza dough of your choice (if you're using Gluten-Free Dough, see the note about it in the introduction to this chapter, page 129)

1 pound (450 g) fresh strawberries, hulled and quartered

CREAM CHEESE ICING

2 ounces (56 g) cream cheese, softened

1 tablespoon (14 g) unsalted butter, softened

⅓ cup (60 g) powdered sugar

1 teaspoon (5 g) milk or cream

¼ teaspoon (1 g) vanilla extract

Flaky salt for sprinkling

TO PREPARE THE SUGAR COATING AND PAN BASE

Preheat the oven to 375°F.

In a small bowl, mix the brown sugar, granulated sugar, cinnamon, and salt.

Lightly brush an 8-by-8-inch square baking dish with 2 tablespoons (28 g) of the melted butter and sprinkle it with half the cinnamon-sugar mixture.

TO PREPARE THE DOUGH

On a lightly floured surface, use your hands to roll the pizza dough into an 8-inch log.

Use a sharp knife to slice the log in half lengthwise, then cut each half into 8 equal pieces and roll each one into a ball. You should have 16 dough balls.

Set up a little assembly line with the remaining 3 tablespoons (43 g) of melted butter and the remaining cinnamon-sugar mixture. Dip each dough ball into the melted butter, then roll it in the sugar mixture until fully coated.

Spread the quartered strawberries over the sugar base in the pan.

Layer the coated dough pieces over the strawberries in a 4-by-4 grid, loosely packed. Bake for 25 to 30 minutes, or until puffed and golden brown on top.

TO MAKE THE CREAM CHEESE ICING

While the monkey bread bakes, whisk together the cream cheese, butter, powdered sugar, milk, and vanilla in a small bowl until smooth.

Once out of the oven, let the monkey bread rest for 2 to 3 minutes. Then gently press the sides inward with a spatula to loosen. Invert the pan onto a plate or tray so the sticky, caramelized bottom becomes the top.

Sprinkle flaky salt over the top and serve warm with the cream cheese icing on the side or drizzled directly over the monkey bread.

HOT FUDGE SAUCE

The first six months of Square Pie Guys' brick and mortar existence were simultaneously the most exhilarating and stressful of my entire life. It was an absolute thrill to watch my tiny pop-up transform into an actual restaurant filled with actual customers, but every day brought new challenges to overcome, new skills to quickly acquire, and so much more to worry about than when it was just me, a portable oven, and a stack of Lloyd pans. Some people might cope with this kind of daily cortisol overload by meditating, but my approach was to hunch over the bar at the end of service and self-soothe by double-fisting spoonfuls of this rich, chocolatey hot fudge sauce and ice-cold glass bottles of Miller High Life. Would a doctor or therapist recommend this approach to self-care? Probably not, but I can attest that it got the job done.

This sauce is also great over ice cream.

YIELD: ABOUT 1½ CUPS

1 cup (240 g) heavy cream

½ cup (160 g) light corn syrup

⅓ cup (67 g) dark brown sugar

¼ cup (25 g) unsweetened cocoa powder (preferably Dutch-process)

¼ teaspoon (1.5 g) fine sea salt

6 ounces (170 g) semisweet or bittersweet chocolate (60 to 70 percent), chopped

2 tablespoons (28 g) unsalted butter

1 teaspoon (5 g) pure vanilla extract

In a medium saucepan over medium heat, whisk together the cream, corn syrup, brown sugar, cocoa powder, and salt until smooth and just starting to bubble around the edges.

Reduce the heat to low, stir in the chopped chocolate and butter, and continue stirring until everything is melted and silky.

Let it gently simmer (not boil) for 3 to 4 minutes, stirring frequently. It'll thicken a bit as it cooks.

Remove from the heat, stir in the vanilla, and let it sit for 5 minutes before serving. It will thicken more as it cools.

NOTE: THE HOT FUDGE KEEPS WELL IN AN AIRTIGHT CONTAINER IN THE FRIDGE FOR UP TO 2 WEEKS. REHEAT GENTLY IN THE MICROWAVE OR ON THE STOVE WITH A SPLASH OF CREAM OR MILK TO LOOSEN.

ITALIAN-STYLE DOUGHNUTS WITH ORANGE SUGAR

These doughnuts start with pizza dough but get the zeppole treatment, rolled in fragrant orange sugar while still warm. They couldn't be easier to make, but the results taste like something from a Roman street fair. Perfect with espresso or served in a paper bag and eaten on the go. However you serve them, don't be surprised if they disappear instantly.

YIELD: 6 TO 12 DOUGHNUTS, DEPENDING ON SIZE

ORANGE SUGAR COATING

½ cup (100 g) granulated sugar

Zest of 1 large orange (about 1 tablespoon or 4 g)

Pinch of kosher salt

DOUGHNUTS

All-purpose flour for dusting

10 ounces (280 g) pizza dough of your choice (if you're using Gluten-Free Dough, see the note about it in the introduction to this chapter, page 129)

Neutral oil for frying (such as canola, sunflower, or grapeseed); about 2 cups (475 g) for shallow frying

TO PREPARE THE ORANGE SUGAR COATING

In a shallow bowl, combine the granulated sugar, orange zest, and salt. Use your fingers to rub the zest into the sugar until fragrant and well mixed. Set aside.

TO MAKE THE DOUGHNUTS

On a lightly floured surface, divide the dough into 12 small or 6 medium equal-size pieces. You can pinch off pieces by hand for a more rustic shape. Lightly roll them into balls or shape into doughnut rings, being careful not to overwork the dough.

Pour about 2 inches of oil into a heavy-bottomed pot or deep skillet. Heat to 350°F, using a thermometer if you have one. If not, test with a small dough scrap: It should sizzle and rise to the top quickly.

Carefully drop a few pieces of dough into the hot oil at a time, being careful not to overcrowd. Fry for 2 to 3 minutes per side, or until golden brown and puffed. Use a slotted spoon to transfer them to a paper towel–lined plate.

While the doughnuts are still warm (but not too hot to handle), roll them in the orange sugar mixture until fully coated.

Best enjoyed immediately, while crisp on the outside and steamy inside. If you want to really gild the lily, serve with warm Hot Fudge Sauce (page 145) for dipping.

ACKNOWLEDGMENTS

TO RICHARD ABATE AND HANNAH CARANDE AT 3ARTS

For your belief in this project from the start and all the work you did to make it happen.

TO EDWARD ASH-MILBY

For your creative partnership and editorial guidance.

TO MEG SINEAD BINGHAM, STACY VENTURA, VICTORIA WOOLLARD, ALLEE CAKMIS, AND MARCELL TURNER

For your keen design, excellent styling, and gorgeous photography. Your contributions brought my story and recipes to life so beautifully.

TO GABI

For pushing me to do this book and for helping bring it to life.

TO JEFF NEWMAN

For telling me I could not make great pizza at home, then handing me your pizza stone and Jim Lahey's *No-Knead Pizza* book anyway. That contradiction started everything.

TO LAUREN (JEFF'S WIFE)

For the squares hate. Your relentless trolling of my square pizzas pushed me to lean in and own it. That is how "Square Pie Guy" was born, and eventually Square Pie Guys. Thank you for the unintended branding assist.

TO THE PIZZA COMMUNITY AND SOCIAL MEDIA

For sharing knowledge freely and giving me confidence before I had any credentials. Thank you to the pizza makers who responded to DMs from a total stranger in 2016 (shout-out to Scottie Rivera). The generosity of this community changed my life.

TO TOM GOZNEY

That first Roccbox made it possible to cook restaurant-quality pizzas consistently and for me to build a real pop-up. That little green oven was a game-changer.

TO THE POP-UP DAYS

In the early days, it was just me and my former business partner, Danny, building pop-ups from scratch. Long days, big energy, and the feeling that something special was happening. I will always be grateful for that chapter and what we built together.

TO OUR EARLY POP-UP SUPPORTERS

Zeitgeist, Anina, Vinyl Wine Bar, the *San Francisco Chronicle* write-up, the Eater nomination, the long lines, and the first real signs that this idea might work. Thank you to everyone who showed up when this was still unproven.

TO MY FRIENDS AND EARLY INVESTORS

Dianne, Varun, Alex, Lou Haidous, Stephen, Tricia, Evan, Charlie, Adrienne, Jonah, and so many others who taste-tested, encouraged, and eventually invested in something that made very little sense at the time. Thank you for believing early.

TO ALL SPG INVESTORS

For taking a bet on Detroit-style pizza in the Bay Area and helping turn a pop-up into a real business.

TO THE TEAM AT SQUARE PIE GUYS, PAST AND PRESENT

You are the real "Guys." This is ours.

TO MY PARENTS AND FAMILY

For teaching me that food is love, that meals matter, and that bringing people together around a table is meaningful work. And thank you for believing in me through the rough seasons.

TO TESS

You have been there for the lowest lows and highest highs, and you handled both better than I did. You steadied me, challenged me, pushed me to think bigger, and reminded me to breathe when I forgot how. You helped me become a better leader and, more importantly, a better man. Square Pie Guys grew up after I met you. So did I. That is not a coincidence. And yes, thank you for making me slightly cooler than I actually am and for quietly retiring most of my old wardrobe.

I LOVE YOU.

YOUR FAVORITE KINDA SQUARES

Cash and good times at my very first pop-up at Lost & Found in Oakland (now closed), 2017.

Doing some R&D in NYC at Joe's Pizza.

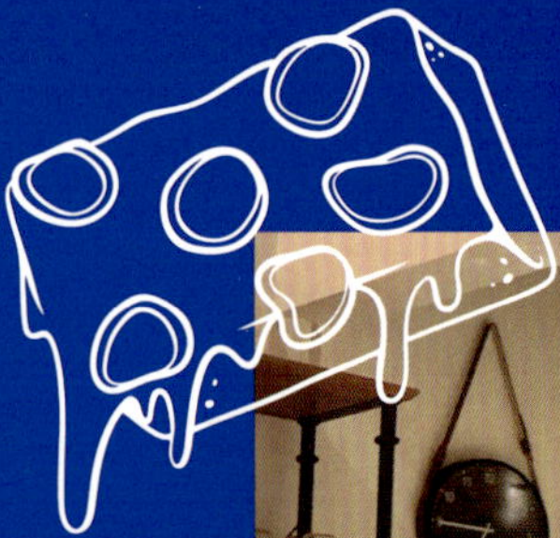

Gino's of Great Neck! My hometown pizzeria and one of the places that inspired my pizza palate—and the inspiration for the North Station Plaza Pie in this book.

SPG IN THE EARLY DAYS!

One of my first pop-ups at Black Hammer Brewing, 2018.

ONE OF THE EARLIEST SPG PIES!!! This was from the wedding I catered at Vinyl Wine Bar in San Francisco—these folks bought my first thirty Detroit pans.

One of the last SPG pop-ups at Vinyl before the first store opened.

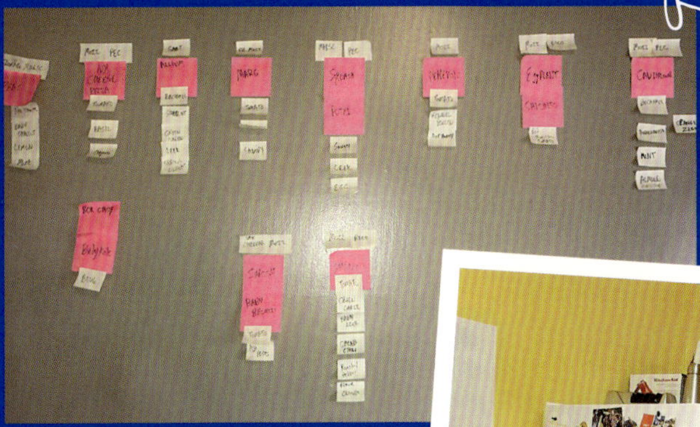

The menu for one of my very first pizza parties in my old Berkeley house in 2016.

PIZZA-MAKING CLASS

First professional photoshoot for Feastly and my first Detroit-Style Pop-Up at Vinyl before Square Pie Guys officially launched.

INDEX

Q

R

S

Marc's Comedy Club

ABOUT THE AUTHOR

Marc Schechter is the owner and founder of Square Pie Guys, a Detroit-style pizzeria in San Francisco. After a career in tech sales, Marc traded the hustle and grind of cold calling and sales quotas for the less secure but more soul-satisfying hustle and grind of making and selling pizza for a living. Marc is a self-taught pizza maker and not your typical chef. He grew up on Long Island, New York, attended college in Miami, and graduated with a job in sales and a plan to work his way up the corporate ladder. But his life took a vastly different turn when he started making pizza in his apartment kitchen in Berkeley, California. He fell in love quickly and began working in several Bay Area pizzerias. Eventually, he started a Detroit-style square-pie pop-up at a San Francisco wine bar. Seven years later, Square Pie Guys is a leading Detroit-style pizzeria in the Bay Area, with six locations. In addition to running the restaurants, Marc manages the @Pizza Instagram account and creates video content for Gozney, a pizza oven brand. He lives in Oakland, California, with his wife, Tess, and their cat, Reuben.

weldon**owen**
an imprint of Insight Editions
P.O. Box 3088
San Rafael, CA 94912
www.weldonowen.com

CEO Raoul Goff
SVP Group Publisher Jeff McLaughlin
VP Publisher Roger Shaw
Associate Publisher Thom O'Hearn
Executive Editor Edward Ash-Milby
Assistant Editor Kayla Belser
Production Editor Ivy Long
Art Director & Designer Megan Sinead Bingham
Designer Gabriella Wikidal
Production Designer Jean Hwang
VP Manufacturing Alix Nicholaeff
Production Manager Deena Hashem
Strategic Production Planner Lina s Palma-Temena

Photography by Stacy Ventura
Food Styling by Victoria Woollard
Food Styling Assistance from Allee Cakmis

Additional photography by Tom Gozney (page 9), Marcell Turner (pages 10, 89, 105, 149), and Feastly (pages 19, 28, 150 bottom left).

Weldon Owen would also like to thank Sheri Linden and Karen Levy, with a special thanks to our hand models, Allee Cakmis, Asa Kittner, and Ben Cardoza.

ISBN: 979-8-88674-435-4

Manufactured in China by Insight Editions
10 9 8 7 6 5 4 3 2 1